Ambiton for Change
Partnership, children and work

Ann Jamieson and Sue Owen

The National Children's Bureau (NCB) works to identify and promote the well-being and interests of all children and young people across every aspect of their lives.

NCB is a registered charity which encourages professionals and policy makers to see the needs of the whole child and emphasises the importance of multidisciplinary, cross-agency partnerships. It has adopted and works within the UN Convention on the Rights of the Child and according to NCB stated values and principles.

It collects and disseminates information about children and promotes good practice in children's services through research, policy and practice development, membership, publications, conferences, training and an extensive library and information service.

Several Councils and Fora are based at NCB and contribute significantly to the breadth of its influence. It also works in partnership with Children in Scotland and Children in Wales and other voluntary organisations concerned for children and their families.

Published by National Children's Bureau Enterprise, the trading company for the National Children's Bureau, Registered Charity number 258825.

ISBN 1 900990 52 0

© National Children's Bureau, 2000
8 Wakley Street, London EC1V 7QE

Typeset by LaserScript, Mitcham, Surrey

Printed by Biddles Ltd, Guildford, Surrey

Contents

About the authors

Ann Jamieson is Director of the Early Childhood Unit, NCB.

Sue Owen is Principal Development Officer at the Early Childhood Unit, NCB.

The **Early Childhood Unit** is a widely respected body in the early years field. Previous publications include *Quality in Diversity* (NCB Enterprises, 1998), *Planning, Partnership and Equality for Young Children* (NCB Enterprises, 1998) *Tuning in to Children* (BBC Educational Developments, 1997), *Not Just a Nursery* (NCB Enterprises, 1997), *Communication Between Babies in their First Year* (NCB Enterprises, 1996), *Managing to Change* (NCB Enterprises, 1995), *Child Development from Birth to Eight* (NCB Enterprises, 1993) and the videos *Heuristic Play with Objects* (NCB Enterprises, 1992) and *Infants at Work* (NCB Enterprises, 1986).

Preface

This publication from the Early Childhood Unit at the National Children's Bureau gives an analysis of the early years development and childcare partnerships and plans derived from a record of the Unit's involvement in policy and practice nationally, regionally and locally, from May 1997 to August 1999.

Our concern has been to gain an understanding of the contribution of the partnerships to the continuing quest to balance work and the bringing up of children for both women and men. In doing so, it has been our pleasure to identify many of the voices that have brought us to this momentous point of departure.

Ann Jamieson and Sue Owen

Acknowledgements

This book is about partnership and we would like to acknowledge the support and resources we have had from colleagues at all stages. We are grateful to the five local authorities and their representatives for permission to use their case studies in the report of the Audit/Partnership Project. Similarly to the other core partners in the project for their development work with us: National Childminding Association, Working for Childcare and the Department of Applied Social Studies and Social Research at the University of Oxford. Our thanks also to Reggio Children for permission to reproduce the 'Laura' photos. We always owe a debt of gratitude to the local authority coordinators and partnership officers who attend the national and regional meetings of the Coordinators' Network for the sophisticated and honest debate which they allow to take place. We are also grateful to the many civil servants who have worked on these initiatives over the past two years and who have attended meetings and shared with us the development of their work.

We would also like to thank the staff of the Early Childhood Unit for their support in completing this publication, particularly Ann Robinson, Gemma Stunden and Pat Thomas. Also, thanks to the publications and marketing staff at NCB and our colleague Claire Cordeaux of the HERA 2 project.

Working in partnership

Working in partnership is an Early Childhood Unit facilitated development programme for Early Years Development and Childcare Partnerships. It is organised around a series of six inter-related workshops each of which is designed to enable partnership members and servicing officers to explore their shared and separate responsibilities in some depth.

Each workshop will consider national, local and regional expectations. By the end of the process, the partnership members are expected to have successfully worked together to produce their own partnership-specific materials which link clearly and directly to national guidance, but which clearly reflect local wishes and expectations.

Early Childhood Unit lead, facilitate and record all discussion. They then produce a set of partnership-specific materials at the end of the process which will be the property of the partnership.

Introduction

'But the practice of everything new however trifling require time and experience to perfect it. It cannot be expected that arrangements which comprehend the whole business of life and reduce to practice the entire science of political economy can at once be combined and executed in the best manner. Many errors will be at first committed; and as in every other attempt by human means to unite a great many of the parts to produce one grand result many partial failures may be anticipated.'

Robert Owen (1836)

For the past two years we have been working with our colleagues in local, central and regional government and across the country in the Early Years Development and Childcare Partnerships to help make sense of the best ways in which people can bring up their children. Primarily our interest is in young children but our concern has always been to relate early childhood to the conditions of society in the broadest terms. This work has led us to think that there is serious ambition to unite the economic, social, cultural and physical aspects of life into a way of putting children first rather than leaving them to absorb inequality as has been the pattern for so long. Our argument is that this is a whole child, whole society task. 'It takes a whole country to educate a child' might be our version of the often-quoted African proverb.

The quest for convergence and inclusion in our massively disparate world is real and, in our experience, is alive and well within the new partnerships. There are many policy agendas being driven by central government which impinge on the lives of children all of which are evident explicitly or implicitly in the work of the partnerships. Furthermore, in tackling local regeneration and capacity building, the partnerships confront some of the most difficult political and economic issues shared by nation-states around the world.

Much of the rhetoric in early years and childcare over the past decade has related to the need for integration and organisational coherence and this is evident in the changes which have been made most recently. However in considering the strings of action and reaction which have brought the UK to this particular point of departure we have been struck more by the arguments which have not been put than by those which appear to have been won. The history of early years and childcare services is not one of incoherence or dysfunction but rather one of the bubbling up of the most powerfully held beliefs and values and the persistent inability of government to resolve the fundamental relationship between economics and the bringing up of children.

The present day partnerships have come into existence as a consequence of this dilemma. Because of this they offer an opportunity to set out the arguments about the reconciliation of work and the bringing up of children which should not be missed. An examination of the conditions in which the notion of 'partnership' and the administrative expression of this in the partnerships should therefore be a national priority in our view.

We believe that it is the power of argument and the extent to which they are able to reflect the realities of peoples lives which will in the end determine the effectiveness of the partnerships. What follows is, therefore, an examination of our own evidence of the fitness for purpose of existing structures and of emergent models here and in other parts of the world which offer vision for the future. In so doing we have taken some inspiration from the pioneer industrialist and philosopher Robert Owen whose mills at New Lanark in Scotland have served as an exemplar of good practice since the 1800s. Owen's quotes are to be found in much of the literature of early years and childcare but he is just as relevant to works on economic regeneration. Our introductory quote, for example, is to be found in the Gulbenkian Foundation publication *At the Heart of the Community Economy* (Pearce, 1993). The following quote is from *Transforming Nursery Education* (Moss and Penn, 1996).

> If left to their own impulses, children fill the air with perpetual questionings. Every new thing being a mystery to them, their demands for information are co-extensive with novelty. Rational children should not be stinted, rebuked or dispirited [but allowed] a continuous elastic spirit, ever inquiring and ever extending to others the fullness of its own aspirations.
>
> *Robert Owen (1836)*

1 The story so far...

'My mummy works, so does my daddy.' *(Lucy, aged four)*

In 1972 Margaret Thatcher, then Secretary of State for Education, issued a White Paper, *Education: A framework for expansion* (Department of Education and Science, 1972), which promised a nursery education place for all four-year-old children whose parents wanted one, within a ten-year period. That promise was not implemented. Only in 1996, 24 years later, did another Conservative Government, unpopular and fast approaching an election, introduce a voucher-based scheme designed to deliver such places in a manner which marks the beginning of today's partnership-based, mixed-economy approach.

To have the fullest understanding of the influences which have brought us to this point, it is necessary to retrace the past to the beginnings of industrial society, depicted in the table on p. 2. Robert Owen was experimenting with extraordinarily progressive provision in the early 1800s but, within his lifetime, children were also being separated from their parents in the Victorian workhouses in cruel and demeaning ways. This said, we are only able to consider the seminal events of the past fifty years in this study. What this table shows, nonetheless, is the uneven and precarious development with clear evidence of large themes being acted out in the name of the nation's children. Our story begins with the inception of the welfare state and continues in seesawing fashion up to the present day.

It hardly needs saying here that great events followed the end of the Second World War as far as welfare delivery was concerned: the Welfare State, the NHS, the Beveridge Plan and the 1948 Children Act. Perhaps less well remembered, 1948 also brought in the Nurseries' and Child-Minders' Regulation Act. This was passed in an attempt to impose standards on childcare for workers' children. During the Second World War, the state had run nurseries to enable women to enter the workforce, but was not prepared to maintain this expenditure after the war. It was envisaged that companies would take over the nurseries, if they needed

Table 1.1 The story so far . . .

1948	Nurseries and Childminders' Regulation Act
1960	Circular 8/60, Ministry of Education specifically discourages local authorities from setting up new nursery education in order to ensure the supply of teachers for older children
1961	Setting up of the Pre-school Playgroups Association (PPA) by parents running nursery education groups for their own children, in response to the Government's ban on local authority spending in this area
1967	Central Advisory Council for Education Report, *Children and their Primary Schools* (the Plowden Report), outlined current thinking on the importance of play for the education of young children but resolved that full time nursery education should not be provided as a means of enabling women to work
1968	Educational Priority Areas Programme established a series of Priority Area Playgroups to bring the advantages of pre-school experience to young children in disadvantaged areas using community development methods which involved their parents and their communities
1968	Nurseries and Childminders' Regulation Act 1948 was amended to make it more appropriate for the main categories of day care which had expanded since the Second World War, that is, childminding and playgroups
1970	Setting up of the Community Development Projects by the Home Office to test the approach as a means of combating disadvantage
1971	Setting up of unified social services departments in England following the Seebohm Report (1968). Childcare officers then became generic social workers and social services departments took over from health visitors in implementing the Nurseries and Child-minders' Regulations with some local authorities establishing new posts of under-fives officers to do this work
1972	The White Paper, *Education: A framework for expansion*, promised a state-funded nursery education place for all four-year-olds
1973	Nursery Education Circular (Department of Education and Science, 1973)
1975	Children Act passed which addressed concerns over the failure of the state to protect children, such as Maria Colwell, by limiting the rights of parents
1977	National Childminding Association established, following a BBC Television training series for childminders, *Other People's Children*
1978	Voluntary Organisations Liaison Council for Under Fives (VOLCUF) set up, following an initiative by Lady Plowden. It later became the National Early Years Network
1980	Education Act begins a period of rapid change to include the National Curriculum, Local Management of Schools, Standard Assessment Tests and league tables
1980	National Childcare Campaign established (later evolving into The Day Care Trust).
1983	DHSS Under-Fives Initiative funded a large number of voluntary sector early years projects including a small grants scheme
1984	House of Commons Social Services Committee under Renée Short reported on the provision made for children in public care and lamented the disproportionately low amounts spent on preventative work

1984   Workplace Nursery Campaign was started

1985   Various local authorities, starting with Strathclyde, began to set up integrated or combined services for young children with corresponding management structures within local government

1986   Under-Fives Unit (now the Early Childhood Unit) established at the National Children's Bureau

1987   The Report of the Cleveland Inquiry chaired by Elizabeth Butler-Sloss

1988   House of Commons Education, Science and Arts Committee report, *Educational Provision for the Under Fives*, includes arguments on the need for educational provision, current quality and good practice. Coordination and involvement of parents

1988   The Education Reform Act

1989   The Children Act was passed, described as the most comprehensive piece of legislation for children and intended to be holistic, requiring that local authorities act corporately to ensure effective strategic planning of a comprehensive and inclusive nature. Provisions included: services for children in need and their families with the proviso that children were best cared for within their own homes; family support as a broad system of services intended to reflect local needs including day care; joint education/social services triennial reviews of day care and related services; and, following active cross-sector lobbying, new provisions on registration and inspection of early years services including education in day care settings

1989   Second DHSS Under-Fives Initiative

1990   *Starting with Quality* was the report for the DES of the Committee of Inquiry into the Quality of Educational Experience Offered to Three- and Four-Year-Olds, chaired by Angela Rumbold MP. The Committee outlined what it believed to be essential elements in play-based education for young children and the rights of all children to such provision, but which were explicitly shunned by the then Government

1990   Working for Childcare established to continue the Workplace Nursery Campaign

1992   Local Authority Early Years Coordinators' Network set up by the Early Childhood Unit to offer a national discussion and updating forum

1992   European Council of Ministers' recommendation to address the need for a wide range of family provision to support parents in the reconciliation of employment and family life

1992   NVQs in Childcare and Education launched, following the work of the Under-Sevens Project set up in 1989 to map the occupational competencies in the early years sector

1993   First integrated early years degrees offered at Suffolk College and the University of Bristol

1993   National Commission on Education Report, *Learning to Succeed*

1993   Government announced first of two funding initiatives to set up out-of-school provision, administered by TECs

1993   European Commission White Paper, *Growth, Competitiveness and Employment: Challenges and ways forward into the 21st century*

1994   European Commission White Paper, *European Social Policy: A way forward for the Union.*

1994   *The Importance of Early Learning* (the Start Right Report) by Sir Christopher Ball for the Royal Society of Arts

1994	*Seen but Not Heard*, Audit Commission report on child health and social services for children in need highlighted the need for a more collaborative approach by statutory agencies and the role of day care in prevention
1994	Childcare Still a Trades Union Issue, Working for Childcare Conference
1995	Childcare Disregard established as part of the benefits system to encourage more mothers of young children to enter the workforce
1995	*Child Protection: Messages from research*, Department of Health report collating the findings of research studies into child protection
1996	*Counting to Five*, Audit Commission report on their local evaluations of early years services with recommendations on how to improve future planning and auditing
1996	Department of Health initiative, Refocusing Children's Services, with the aim of ensuring that child protection is firmly placed within the context of wider work to support children in need and their families by avoiding too narrow a focus on alleged incidents of abuse or neglect. £700,000 allocated in grant aid to specific projects exemplifying this approach. This was designed to address the fact that the Children Act had not resulted in the expected change from crisis-led to preventative work
1996	Nursery Education and Grant Maintained Schools Act
1996	Phase One of Nursery Education Vouchers: four local authorities volunteer to try out the scheme for a year and a new inspectorate is set up under OFSTED to assess the ability of funded providers to meet new Desirable Learning Outcomes by the time children are aged five
1996	Cheryl Gillan, Minister for Education and Employment, announced a consultation paper on developing a national framework for childcare, *Work and Family Life: Ideas and options for childcare*, incorporating principles of availability, affordability, accessibility, quality and coherence and involving a range of key players, such as parents, employers, TECs, local authorities and the private and voluntary sectors
1996	*Early Excellence: A head start for every child*, Shadow Cabinet statement intimating abolition of vouchers and the setting up of Early Excellence Centres and Early Years Plans following a consultation exercise conducted by Margaret Hodge MP
1997	Labour Government elected: Early Years Development Plans and Partnerships (EYDPs) are set up instead of the voucher scheme First Early Years Development Plans are required by 1 January 1999
1998	School Standards and Framework Act included a statutory requirement to set up partnerships and write Early Years Development and Childcare Plans Second round of Early Excellence Centre applications Consultation on a review of regulation and inspection to meet criticisms about duplication of systems and conflicting standards
1998	Consultation on the Review of the Desirable Learning Outcomes by the Qualifications and Curriculum Agency (QCA) Consultation on a National Training and Qualifications Framework developed by the QCA National Training Organisations (NTOs) set up for Early Years and Playwork. National Childcare Strategy announced and consulted on

1998	Working Families' Tax Credit announced as a way of allowing working parents to pay for childcare in the private market
	Comprehensive Spending Review on services for the under-sevens leads to the announcement of the Sure Start programme to support vulnerable children under age three (interdepartmental)
	Quality Protects initiative and funding for social services departments
	Childcare Audits are required as part of the Early Years Development and Childcare Plans
	New Early Years Development and Childcare Partnerships set up based on the EYDPs

1999	First Early Years Development and Childcare Plans completed by 1 February 1999
	Sure Start applications completed by 20 March 1999
	Third round Early Excellence Centre applications completed 23 April 1999
	Press release announced the findings of the review of regulation and inspection in August: OFSTED to take over all inspection arrangements, £30 million released to improve ratios in reception classes and a pilot programme of higher ratios instituted for some voluntary and private settings
	Revised Guidance for Early Years Development and Childcare Plans issued in September
	Working Families' Tax Credit came into effect in October

women workers, and that there should be some state control of standards. In fact, the main increase in post-war provision was in childminding.

At the same time, the major problem facing successive ministers of education was the shortage of teachers which led to Circular 8/60 in 1960:

> The Minister cannot encourage authorities to propose any new nursery schools or any enlargement of nursery schools in the case of nursery classes. The Minister is especially concerned to ensure that teachers are not diverted from the teaching of older children.
>
> *van der Eyken (1973) p. 432*

As a result, such was the concern of essentially middle-class parents that a new national movement called The Pre-school Playgroups Association began to evolve.

Expansion became possible in 1972. With the White Paper, *Education: A framework for expansion*, followed by a Circular on Nursery Education in 1973, Margaret Thatcher began to implement the recommendations of the Central Advisory Council for Education report *Children and their Primary Schools* (Plowden Report, 1967). The Circular advocated a ten-year expansion and aimed at making two years of sessional nursery education available for all children before entering school, where their parents wanted this. There was a clear emphasis on the benefits of nursery education as a means of 'reducing educational and social disadvantages'. However, it must be noted that, above all, the Plowden Report set the seal on the identification of nursery education as preparation for primary school with the proviso that such provision should be sessional and not designed to accommodate children all day.

This policy came at a time when, following the Seebohm Report (Ministry of Housing and Local Government, 1968), social services departments were being formed as a unified means of delivering personal assistance across the board to both old and young. There was the 'rediscovery of poverty' and a push on the part of policy analysts to determine the best means of identifying and quantifying need. Educational Priority Areas, for instance, had been advocated by the Plowden Report and were to be identified using objective criteria based on available data, rather than on the impressions of experts. The criteria agreed upon were:

- the proportion of unskilled or semi-skilled manual workers;
- family size;
- use of state supplements such as free school meals;
- overcrowded housing;
- poor attendance/truancy;
- proportion of children with special needs;
- incomplete families;
- children unable to speak English.

The projects incorporated the practices of community development work into the preventative strategies of social services departments and early years interventions, particularly community-run playgroups, were often part of such strategies. As Connor explained (1971), when describing the Liverpool EPA, the aim was to use the practice of parent involvement (pioneered as a way of staffing playgroups in more advantaged areas) in order to weave education into the lives of the disadvantaged:

> Parents are needed, that is the first requisite, they respond to the need and find themselves seeing children in a new light. The learning atmosphere is all around them and they have time to join in.
>
> *E Connor (1971) p. 15*

In many ways, the recommendations on nursery education in 1973 formed a lowest common denominator. There had been many divergent strands of argument for and against nursery education for over a century. As we have seen, Robert Owen argued that the economic or productive success of his mills at New Lanark rested largely on an approach to the education of children which celebrated each individual's instinctive impulses to enquire and extend to others 'the fullness of its own aspirations'. Serious voices after the Second World War argued for a comprehensive set of policies which could have added up to a national strategy to support the bringing up of children. There were also great swings of policy on the purpose and implementation of nursery education over the years, later augmented by strong voices from the voluntary and parental sectors such as the Pre-School Playgroups Association and the Voluntary Organisations Liaison Council for Under Fives (VOLCUF). Even so, the targets for expansion set in the 1973 Circular were never met and, by 1976, both the Department of Health and the Department of Education had begun to look at the cost of under-fives care.

The 1975 Children Act, hailed by some as a Children's Charter, reduced the power of individual parents in favour of state intervention, making it easier for parental rights to be removed. Criticisms at the time were that the overall impact of the act would be to promote an anti-parent ethos within local government and other state agencies. It was also argued that individual tragedies such as the Maria Colwell case had much more influence than the available research. It is also worth remembering that a succession of inquiries into cases such as Maria Colwell repeatedly identified a tragic lack of inter-agency liaison and collaboration.

A series of Education Acts starting in 1980 was set to change the organisation of education at local level, dramatically culminating in the Education Reform Act (1988). This devolved power to individual schools through the Local Management of Schools, a system which delegates budgets and financial management to the heads and governing bodies of individual institutions rather than resting with a monolithic local education authority. But national centralism replaced local centralism via the establishment of a National Curriculum in 1989 and national standards of inspection implemented by OFSTED in 1993. Throughout all this, the provision of nursery education remained discretionary for LEAs. This undoubtedly contributed to the extremely uneven distribution of early years provision across Britain, which was to characterise services up to the present day.

Parallel to the developments within nursery education were those taking place in day care. The amendments to the 1948 Nurseries and Child-minders' Regulation Act in 1968 had shown public acknowledgment of the growth and importance of childminding as the major form of provision for children with working parents. However, a number of studies in the 1970s highlighted cases of poor childminding care which were taken up and sensationalised by the press. The lobbying and support activities which resulted from this culminated in the National Childminding Association in 1977 as a professional organisation run by and for childminders. It also, as the name implies, provides services for anyone with an interest in childminding, including local authority officers and parents.

Day nursery provision was slower to grow and, indeed, the number of places in local authority-run nurseries declined consistently after the Second World War, until they were serving almost exclusively children in need referred by social workers. However, it was recognised to be undesirable to concentrate children with problems in one form of provision. This, coupled with the lack of places, resulted in some local authorities choosing to purchase day care places for children in need from regular providers, such as private and community nurseries, child-minders and playgroups.

The 1970s had also seen a movement towards community-run day nurseries and these formed the basis for the work of the National Childcare Campaign, which was set up in 1980 to support the development of such nurseries and to fight for accessible and affordable early years services in general. These services have evolved into the Day Care Trust. Nevertheless, the real growth in group day care was in the private day nursery sector in the 1980s, in response to the needs of working parents who could afford unsubsidised fees. In England, places in private day nurseries rose from 22,017 in 1980 to 57,669 in 1990 (DoH, 1990). There was even a significant growth in employer support for working parents at this time, although the number of companies actually providing nurseries on site was still very limited.

The year 1983 saw the DHSS set up the first of two under-fives initiatives. These took the form of several separately funded projects, many of which prefigured present-day policy. Perhaps most notably, the first Children's Information Service was set up under this initiative in Sheffield, after civil servants had visited the resource and referral services which were widespread in the United States. This was seen as a cheap route to the improvement of early years provision by ensuring that consumers had better information about what already existed and therefore would be in a better position to demand more quality and quantity of service.

It is important to note that, despite the move to unify services for individually vulnerable families in the Seebohm reforms of the early seventies, services were still very distinctly compartmentalised and inequality was growing. The innovations within the community development projects and the education priority areas to develop community-based centres, which included a full range of services, did not have the influence which was originally envisaged, despite the successes of individual programmes.

Against this background, the conclusions of the House of Commons Social Services Committee Report (1984) were both timely and extremely revealing. This inquiry into the provision for children in public care in England and Wales evidenced widespread concern, supporting this quote from its Chair, Renée Short:

> If half the funds and the intellectual effort which has gone towards developing strategies for finding alternative families had been put into what we can only lamely call preventative work, there would be unquestionable advantage to all concerned.

Not much later, in 1988, Elizabeth Butler-Sloss, the judge who chaired the Cleveland Inquiry, was drawn to conclude that 'Children must be seen as people not objects of concern' following the removal of children from their homes who had had inappropriately invasive and inaccurate examinations to detect evidence of sexual abuse. Cleveland was probably the largest so-called child abuse scandal in a long series of cases which contributed to a climate of moral panic and the vilification of social workers in the media.

Around this time, it is also important to record the influence of the drive for equality, especially from the women's movement. This could be seen in the formation of what was to become the day care lobby with pressure groups, such as the Workplace Nursery Campaign, leading the field. Similar influence can also be seen to be at work at local authority level. Here, throughout the late eighties and early nineties, several authorities began to develop integrated services for young children and their families. Strathclyde, Southwark, Manchester, Sheffield and others all confronted diverse aspects of change, including those arising from combining separate professional practice and discourse. In their own way, these services pioneered the present-day modernisation and Best Value agenda. They also served to provide a focus at local level for the equality agenda of both the women's movement and the poverty lobby; this was particularly true of the extensive expansion in early years activity which took place in the 1980s under the influence of the GLC's Women's Committee. After the GLC was disbanded, some of the funding for London-wide childcare support organisations continued to be provided by the London Boroughs Grants Committee.

Then, in 1989, the Children Act was launched as the 'most comprehensive piece of legislation this century to affect children'. Significantly for our purposes, this Act had at its heart the provision of support services for children in need and their families which was intended to prevent the need for other interventions. It was made clear that such services should not be directly offered as a last resort to stop, for example, reception into care. Department of Health guidance (1991) stressed that:

> Local authorities are not expected to meet every individual need, but they are asked to identify the extent of need and then make decisions on the priorities for service provision in their area in the context of that information and their statutory duties ... Local authorities must comprehensively overhaul existing childcare policies and strategies ... Services should be provided in a non-stigmatising way ... Provision of services should enhance the parents' authority ... Children should participate in decision-making ... Service provision should be sensitive to the needs of members of minority ethnic groups.

The Act also indicated the type of service which might be provided:

- advice, guidance and counselling;
- occupational, social, cultural or recreational activities;
- home helps and laundry;
- travel to services;
- holidays;
- family centres;
- day care, out-of-school and holiday activities.

DoH (1991)

Local authorities were also required within the new arrangements to produce a joint Social Services and Education Review of all day care services for children and their families.

At the time, various models were created within which local authorities could engage in the continuums of planning needed to effect the considerable shifting of priorities and focus which the Act implied. However, the Act did not bring with it new funding or requirements to review budgetary priorities and so there was no significant shift of resources away from crisis-related or 'heavy end' provision. Research from Leicester University by Tunstill and Aldgate (1994) indicated that few authorities actually provided the practical support services envisioned by the Act. A collection of research studies, *Child Protection: Messages from research* commissioned by the Department of Health (Bullock, 1995), was also generally negative about the efficacy of existing interventions.

However, the Act had also served as an opportunity to revise the increasingly out-of-date and much criticised regulation and inspection regime for children's day care. Law Reform for Children's Day Care (a voluntary sector lobby group with local authority input) was the first cross-sectoral lobby group in the early years field and was developed to ensure a consensus on sectoral inputs into the legislative changes. Out of their work in collaboration with the Department of Health came such things as the Section 19 joint reviews, the increase in the age for registration to eight (although interestingly, the group originally argued for the age limit to be 14), annual inspections and equal opportunities clauses.

Close on the heels of the Children Act and prior to its implementation in 1991, the Rumbold Committee of Inquiry, which had considered the quality of the educational experience offered to three- and four-year-olds, recommended that services be characterised as follows (Department of Education and Science, 1990):

- a curriculum for the under-fives;
- planning and implementing the curriculum;
- continuity and progression;
- monitoring, evaluation and review;
- education, training and support for adults working with children;
- organisation and coordination of services;

At this time, the Early Childhood Unit at the National Children's Bureau was articulating the arguments for integration of services and therefore formed the Local Authority Early Years Coordinators' Network in 1992 to support officers who were working across both social services and education departments. A NCB research study, *The Effective Organisation of Early Childhood Services* (McQuail and Pugh, 1995), drew on this network in order to examine some models of good practice and the issues they had raised.

Writing about the developments in integrated services in 1994, a report by the Local Government Management Board quoted a local authority officer responsible for integrated services:

> The problem is that too often people see change as an event which happens at one time. But it's a process, a long hard slog which will never be finished. You have to take people with you. It seems to me that a lot of local authority officers sit around and wait for things to happen. But you've got to make it happen by demonstrating that bits of the service are doing well and that with some support this could happen and not wait for it to happen.
>
> *V Lowndes and K Riley (1994)*

The report listed the following implications for development that highlighted the need:

- for clarity of direction;
- for an approach tailored to the particular needs and priorities of a locality;
- for vision and leadership at both member and officer level;
- for managers and professionals to re-examine old assumptions and traditional ways of doing things;
- to recognise the strength of traditional loyalties and identities among staff;
- to recognise that staff may be fearful of uncertainty and risk;
- to enable staff to work together on specific projects as a way of building new relationships;
- to build on common values among staff;
- for full consultation and information exchange among members, officers, users and external partners;

- to link changes in one set of services with the broader goals of the local authority.

At the time only a few local authorities had chosen to take these large steps of integration, so the issues listed above were not easy, as they questioned basic assumptions about the way in which local authority services operated. As one coordinator put it in a network meeting, 'There was a lot of blood on the stairs and most of it was mine'. However, early years services had an increasingly high profile with politicians, the public and the press and progress in the new services was marked, setting the pace for other developments.

Integration had not kept pace in the field of training and qualifications. The National Nursery Examination Board (NNEB), the major provider of qualifications, was increasingly seen as out-of-date in the current climate, especially in relation to equal opportunities issues. Also, the growth in services involved people, in childminding and playgroups, who were unable to access traditional college-based courses. The Pre-school Playgroups Association (PPA, now PLA) had developed their own training and qualifications over several years and childminders were questioning the appropriateness of some of the courses they were expected to attend, because they had actually been designed for workers in group settings. As a result, many local authorities were designing their own local courses to fill gaps in what was available nationally. Hevey's *The Continuing Under Fives Muddle! An investigation of current training opportunities* (Hevey, 1987) began a debate on how to standardise and improve qualifications across sectors and this culminated in the Local Government Management Board (LGMB) funding the Under-Sevens Project at the National Children's Bureau to develop competencies for National Vocational Qualifications (NVQs) for the early years.

The *Start Right* report on the importance of early learning, produced by the Royal Society of Arts in 1994, presented few surprises for those who were already advocates of early years services. However, it usefully served to provide a comprehensive set of arguments listing, for example, the most persuasive research on outcomes. Not unlike Rumbold, *Start Right* (Ball, 1994) listed the common features it considered essential for early years services:

- clear aims and objectives;
- a broad, balanced and developmentally-appropriate curriculum;
- a variety of learning experiences which are active, relevant and enjoyable;
- the development of warm and positive relationships;

- a well-planned, stimulating, secure and healthy environment;
- a commitment to equal opportunities and social justice.

It also set out the elements of good practice as:

- the integration of education and care;
- unified responsibility for provision;
- targets for growth by a specified year;
- effective and continuing training of early years teachers and carers;
- an appropriate curriculum encouraging active learning and 'purposeful play';
- partnership between parents and educators;
- adequate resources.

However, in listing all the key strands of research, *Start Right* presented perhaps the most comprehensive set of arguments for early years services, quoting to some effect the evidence from the USA that, for every dollar invested, there was a net return in the long term of at least seven times that amount. The argument 'long believed by early years workers' that these savings accrued from the enhanced self-sufficiency of the recipients of the early years interventions began to have more common currency.

It need hardly be said that there remained very distinct boundaries between the different strands of service delivery across health, education and social care evidenced not least by *Seen but Not Heard*, a report on children's services by the Audit Commission (1994), which discussed the need for genuine coordination. This was similar to the findings in *Messages from Research* mentioned above and, later, *Counting to Five*, the report of a national fieldwork study of the state of early years and childcare services, again by the Audit Commission (1996).

External pressures were also beginning to flow from Britain's membership of the European Union. Within the EU, there was the development of the Social Chapter and recommendations from the Council of Ministers in 1992 which proposed a number of specific objectives for the development of services for young children:

- affordability;
- access to services in all areas, both urban and rural;
- access to services for children with special needs, combining safe and secure care with a pedagogical approach;
- close and responsive relations between services and parents and the local communities;

- diversity and flexibility of services;
- increased choice for parents;
- coherence between different sectors.

The European Union Network for the Reconciliation of Family and Employment, which had brought together an expert from each country to discuss, write about and commission studies on the current state of provision in the EU, had been set up in 1986. Its reports highlighted the very patchy provision available to enable parents to reconcile work and family life. Britain came out particularly poorly in this comparison, with its attempts at integration appearing to lag far behind the thinking in other countries where the split between education and care was non-existent. This split was barely even understood as an issue.

EU White Papers in 1993 and 1994 highlighted the need to break down the rigid patterns of gender segregation in the labour force and therefore justified the provision of childcare and family support to enable women to play an equal role in the labour market. They presented an analysis of the relationship between growth, competitiveness and employment and called for a focus on fields of activity with the potential for 'employment-intensive growth', thus justifying the development of childcare and family support as sources of employment in their own right. The White Paper in 1994 also highlighted the fact that women's development is essential to combat not only their own social exclusion but also that of their children.

There was growing awareness of striking shifts in the labour market, with estimates that by the turn of the century more than 70 per cent of the total workforce would be aged between 25 and 49, with increasing numbers of women entering the labour market. Global economic development brought a focus on the phenomenon of jobless growth, with the new digital technologies forcing the pace of change and demanding a highly skilled workforce.

In this climate, central government had begun to sponsor the expansion of out-of-school provision via the Out-of-School Funding Initiative and, amidst pressure from the childcare lobby, introduced Childcare Disregard which was designed to offset some of the costs of childcare fees for low-paid families. At the same time, childcare was becoming a party political issue more than ever before with Gordon Brown the Shadow Chancellor, for example, promising in 1994 to make childcare a fundamental part of economic policy and to enable the 1.5 million lone parents on benefit to find a path into the labour market.

In 1995, the Labour Party in opposition set up an Early Years Task Force chaired by Margaret Hodge, then the new MP for Barking, which was later to produce the Labour party policy document, *Early Excellence: A head start for every child* (Labour Party, 1996). This formed the basis of the Government's manifesto for early years services for the 1997 election and sought to combine several strands of policy at once, namely, those to do with family support, early education, childcare and local regeneration. As Margaret Hodge outlined in an 'opinion piece' in *The Independent* on 3 October 1996, the new emphasis was to be on enabling parents to access all the services they needed in one place:

> We want to do away with the past divisions between education, care and health. Instead of forcing parents to choose between the children they love and the jobs they need, we will provide the opportunity to choose both. Our Early Excellence Centres are the first step in giving the best start to all our children.
>
> *Margaret Hodge*

However, despite the maturity and sophistication of the evidence and the extensiveness of the links to critical policy issues of the day, there was still no overarching central government policy on the provision of childcare, early education and family support, save for that in the Children Act 1989. As we have suggested above, by the mid 1990s, this had foundered on the deficit model operating within most social services departments and the initiative on refocusing children's services was designed to give departments an incentive to do something about the imbalance between crisis and preventative work. Then, just prior to the 1997 general election, John Major introduced the nursery education voucher scheme for four-year-olds. It was finally an attempt to deliver on the earlier Conservative promise of 1972 via the mechanism of education vouchers which parents could spend at the provider of their choice, as long as that provider met the Government's basic quality standards for a nursery education service. Although heavily criticised at the time for its obvious drawbacks, this scheme formalised once and for all the expansion of sessional early years education across the voluntary, maintained and private sectors.

Shortly after the introduction of vouchers, the Conservative Government also introduced a discussion paper entitled *Work and Family: Ideas and options for childcare* (DfEE, 1996) which sought views on the best means of providing childcare to enable parents to enter and maintain themselves within the labour force. However, this did not depart from the assumption that the provision of childcare was essentially the responsibility of parents themselves.

A consensus of intent

By the beginning of 1997, there was a vast literature supporting the integrated development of education, care and family support services.

A clear consensus of intent could be identified across a wide spectrum of national bodies, as the following selection of quotations shows:

> Nursery education for all three- and four-year-olds would be not only expensive, but also inadequate. Increasingly, the research of people like David Farrington shows that the early months, never mind the early years, of a child's life are critical to their life chances. If this is the case, then if we are serious about the creation of a learning society, we need a policy not for nursery education but for comprehensive birth-to-five education and health support.
>
> *M Barber (1996)*

> This approach considers childcare primarily from a labour market perspective but with a focus on driving forward on equal opportunities for women. But the benefits of increasing the supply of good quality childcare stretch beyond the labour market and this must not be forgotten. Developing and stimulating young children is an end in itself and a key element in any childcare policy.
>
> *DfEE (August 1996)*

> A holistic, equal and integrated approach to childcare/nursery and education provision should be advantageous for all the players, particularly the child whatever age, and ultimately the future labour force. In addition, research indicates that children, without some pre-school activity and learning before five years of age, commence primary schooling with an educational disadvantage and often are likely to remain poor achievers. The CBI supports a Government-led national childcare/nursery framework from birth through school years.
>
> *CBI response to the above (October 1996)*

> Flexible working arrangements: consider the use of flexible working to complement both the needs of business and employees, for example:
> - childcare/eldercare (advice/information);
> - on-site nursery or vouchers;
> - maternity/paternity/adoptive leave;
> - job sharing/contract work;
> - part time/term-time working;
> - career breaks;
> - flexible leave (for example, religious holidays).
>
> *CBI Equal Opportunities Statement*

> Nursery education, integrated with support services for children and for their families, gives the best possible start to children academically and socially, and the best opportunity for successful parenting. Access to high quality services must, over time, become available to everyone. Labour will legislate to place a joint duty on local education authorities and social services departments to convene and service an Early Years Forum. This will be a consultative body, charged with reviewing local services for the under-fives and planning their expansion.
>
> *Early Years Services, Shadow Circular, 1/96 (November 1996)*

In parallel with the planned expansion in nursery education, we will embark on a programme to bring education and care into an integrated service, to meet the needs of young children and their families. Our task is to shape services to meet the needs of the child and the family in the 21st century rather than the other way around.

Labour Party (1996)

... the introduction of pre-school education for all four-year-olds whose parents want it and the progressive extension of nursery provision to three-year-olds as resources become available.

Literacy Task Force (1997)

It is self-evident that the physical, intellectual, social and emotional elements of a child's development and well-being are inextricably linked. One can fundamentally affect the others both positively and negatively. High quality educational opportunities cannot be properly utilised by a child who has an undetected medical condition, who is malnourished or who is unable to trust or relate to others in appropriate ways because of abuse or severe early deprivation. Similarly, a child deprived of education in its widest sense will not enjoy the fullest possible social and emotional development. Despite the progress that has undoubtedly been made the development and organisation of local and national services and the training and practice of professionals in all disciplines must recognise this much more than they presently do. This also means that those government departments and services responsible for the physical and material environment in which children develop must give a much higher priority to the problems.

AMA/ACC (1997)

Convergence of opportunity

By May 1997, not only was there this clear consensus of intent and a huge accumulation of evidence from divergent sources about the overwhelming desirability of investing in children's early lives, but also a unique convergence of opportunity for children's services in the emerging rhetoric of the welfare state. In almost every respect, the time was right to forge a new set of relationships to sustain children. The past was full of missed opportunities to reposition the bringing up of children within national priorities and the resultant generation of poor children was the only evidence needed that such prioritisation was fundamental. However, the programme of development has rolled out in a piecemeal, albeit hurried, fashion resting on the policy agenda as set out in *Early Excellence: A head start for every child* and, more recently, on the conclusions of a HM Treasury-led review of services for children from birth to seven (HM Treasury, 1998).

First, there was the reformulation by Labour of the Conservative Government's nursery voucher programme. It led to the abolition of parent-held vouchers, but commitment to the principle of part time nursery education places for all four-year-olds. This was the central feature of Labour's first planning tool, the Early Years Development Plan

(EYDP). Local authority plans for the development of early years services had been a feature of Labour Party policy since the 1992 election. It was seen as a way of forcing low-spending councils to take early years services seriously and commit themselves to a plan of improvement which would gradually change the national patchwork of services and ensure equal access for children in all parts of the country. However, this new planning mechanism was different. Local authorities were not given sole responsibility for the job, they had to share it with local partnerships which included all relevant departments in local authorities, health agencies, the voluntary and private sectors of provision, employers and parents.

The decision to deploy the partnership mechanism in this arena is characteristic of a general approach within the wider context of service delivery. It can be seen to have been at work in early years and childcare, not only in the developing partnership with the voluntary sector, but also between government departments since the 1989 Children Act and in the regeneration actions largely driven by European Union social and economic policy. As such, the concept of partnership is more aspirational than defined, seeking to combine different sectors and members of the public in common cause and mutuality.

The aims of the partnerships within the DfEE guidance, although only demanding a page of text, are nonetheless marked by a subtext of enormous complexity full of both unresolved conflicts and unparalleled opportunity. The implicit political significance of the partnership approach cannot be overstated, juxtaposed as it is to a lack, as yet, of any overarching strategy to support the bringing up of children. Where, for instance, should we situate the recent announcement that Britain is finally allowing for 13 weeks of parental leave? As this is to be unpaid, the likelihood is that take-up will be low and so its role in helping families to reconcile work and family life will be small.

Most of the central strands of government policy interact with the development of early years provision and childcare in some way. The relevant strands can be summed up as: supporting the family; crime reduction strategies; raising standards; reform of the welfare state; equal opportunities; the maintenance of the labour market; reducing social exclusion; and economic policy itself. Childcare will no longer be seen as 'an afterthought or a fringe element of social policies', but as an 'integral part of our economic policy' (Gordon Brown, Chancellor of the Exchequer, July 1997).

The various forms of early years and out-of-school services address these agendas in some obvious ways. However, they also address them in some complex ways, especially given the fact that both the services involved and the social regeneration debate itself are complicated. Not surprisingly, it takes a great deal of time, intelligence and debate to knit them together effectively in any local community and these are luxuries which the current pace of change seems unable to allow us.

Despite the rhetoric on integration and 'joined-up thinking', developments at national level have continued to be characterised by clear differentiations between care, education and play. So that whilst the partnerships carry composite responsibilities, central government continues with compartmentalisation and the maintenance of distinct funding streams for the provision of early years education, the national childcare strategy, tackling social exclusion, supporting the family and the play agenda. Sure Start, for instance, seems to shadow so closely the aims of the Educational Priority Areas of the 1960s that it risks staying, as they did, outside mainstream policy and the aspirations for the bringing up of children which are held by the rest of society. What is also clear is the dominance of the National Childcare Strategy with its targets for expansion which are as yet out of step with other complementary activities, such as the development of the national Training and Qualifications Framework or any effective policy for the recruitment and retention of high-calibre staff.

Whilst completing this review, we have been seriously taken aback to realise just how many times we have been here before and how much of what is seen as innovative today is evident in the practice of the past. At the start of the industrial age, philanthropists like Owen saw the need for comprehensive policies which linked children's needs to those of their parents and the demands of the economy. Since the inception of the welfare state, there have been many experiments and innovations which have given the clearest guidance on how to deliver locally appropriate services with the potential to counter the impact of economic failures. But government has never been able to build on this and set out a grand national policy which links the bringing up of children to economic and civic relationships. As a result, it is families with children who have paid the highest price for the economic survival of society at large.

What, therefore, is the meaning of the designation of delinquent nine-year-olds, pregnant 12-year-olds and 14-year-old fathers as exemplars of the problems in our society? Inequality, unchecked for far too long, has persistently put such children at the very bottom of the heap. Are we surprised that their impoverished environment, which systematically compromises self-expression and the construction of identity, has resulted in such sadness?

Furthermore, what lies behind the overarching ambition of the present Government to create so many childcare places so that women can access the labour market just at the time when the convergence of the newest technologies is changing the nature of paid employment and the institutions which support it? And, as the electorate retreats more and more from the ballot box, the question of whose agenda this is serving is a serious one.

Thus, as we move from 'industrial society' into the 'digital age', history and ideology have given us the early years development and childcare partnerships as political arenas where the relationships which shape children's lives can be reconfigured to everyone's advantage. The question is: can these new and fragile partnerships find the imagination and feeling for humanity which such tasks demand and will they be sufficiently central to the roll-out of government policy to put the bringing up of children at the heart of our civic, social and economic agendas?

2 We're from the Government, we've come to help you!

'We talk glibly of a partnership between statutory and voluntary but with very little doubt who is the junior partner. This, too, has to change. It is time for the statutory services to see themselves as a resource for the voluntary sector, rather than the other way round.'

Dr Maurice Hayes (from van der Eyken, 1987)

The DfEE, which became the lead department for all early years services in 1998, initially placed great emphasis in their presentations on the power and influence to be wielded by partnerships between statutory and voluntary sectors. However, a careful reading of the guidance and an ability to read between lines revealed that the power of partnerships was, in reality, severely restricted. Partnerships were not constituted bodies and had no legal identity through which, for example, to hire staff or handle funds; the LEA set them up, was responsible for writing the early years and childcare plans, reporting on quarterly targets and handling and accounting for government funds. All this had to be done with the full agreement of a properly constituted partnership. Any member of such a partnership could veto the process by contacting the DfEE directly but, given the massive workload for the first plans and the short timescale available to bring the partnerships together, few felt in a position to sabotage their area's chance to obtain unprecedented amounts of funding for an under-resourced service.

The first task of officers in the local authority was to establish the partnerships:

Acknowledging the vital links between care and education, especially in the early years, the Green Paper proposed that the National Strategy should be planned and delivered by local childcare partnerships, building on the existing Early Years Development Partnerships, each of which would then become an Early Years Development and Childcare Partnership.

DfEE (1998a) p. 1

This was initially noted with relief, as there had been fears that the National Childcare Strategy would be entrusted to yet another tier of partnerships or to existing, non-sector organisations such as TECs and there had been some lobbying against this.

The guidance quoted above listed the local authority functions in servicing the partnership. This included convening meetings, arranging accommodation, providing a secretariat, providing background information, facilitating consultation and providing practical support. The membership of the partnerships was prescribed, an independent chair was advocated, suggested day-to-day operations were outlined and so was a method for representation, that is, partnership members should reflect the knowledge and expertise of their constituency without promoting its vested interests. The partnerships were expected to act in the best interests of the local community as a whole, rather than of individual stakeholders.

It was stated that responsibility for drawing up the plan lay with the local authority, but that this must be supported and informed by the partnership as a whole. The partnership should assist in the drawing up of the plan; they must agree it prior to local authority committee approval, at which point no amendments should be made without partnership approval; plans not approved in this way would be referred back to the local authority and, finally, the local authority should work with the partnership in implementing the plan. In advance of legislation, none of this could be enforced but the DfEE used the language of enforcement and, indeed, most local authority officers attempted to follow the prescription.

However, the legal status and responsibilities of the partnerships did raise questions in the 1999–2000 planning period. A meeting arranged between the Early Years Coordinators' Network and the DfEE to clarify their status, prior to the issuing of new guidance, led to the DfEE admitting that the issue had been deliberately fudged in an attempt to ensure that partnerships felt powerful enough to engage in the hard work required during the first year. The 2000–2001 guidance (DfEE, 1999a) contains a clearer outline of the relationship between central and local government and the partnerships, making it more explicit that the local authority holds the main responsibility for the work. The situation of local authorities is, however, undergoing rapid changes as a result of other government agendas and the new guidance does not discuss these new relationships being established between local authorities and communities which are part of the local government modernisation and Best Value agendas being developed by the Department of Environment, Transport and the Regions (DETR). The latter would seem to be essential to the effective functioning of public/private partnerships which are charged with developing community services such as this.

Aims of the partnerships

The aims of the partnerships were listed in the 1999–2000 guidance, as follows:

> The main aim of the Partnership, with the local authority, will be to draw up and agree a Plan which meets the needs of children and parents and to monitor progress against standards. To this end, the Partnership should:
>
> - ensure that the Plan enhances the care, play and educational experience of young children and the care and play experience of children up to age 14, including those with special educational needs and those with disabilities;
> - bring together the maintained, private and voluntary sectors in a spirit of cooperation and genuine partnership, based on existing good practice;
> - be directed by the diverse needs and aspirations of children locally, and of their parents, and pay attention to the support of families;
> - be further directed by the requirements of the local labour market and the needs of local employers, seeking advice from the local Training and Enterprise Council as appropriate;
> - generate genuine partnership and debate between all providers and others, and seek agreement about how needs can best be met;
> - recognise that the private and voluntary sectors have particular strengths;
> - recognise that these sectors often give support to, and in turn, are supported by, parents;
> - understand the reality of the constraints on the local authority, both financial and other; and
> - pay regard to value for money, taking both cost and quality into account, including recognition that the majority of childcare provision normally will be, or will become, financially viable within a short period.
>
> *DfEE (1998a)*

However, the overall aim of the exercise was perhaps best explained by the somewhat different guidance issued to partnerships in Scotland:

> Given the Government's vision that childcare and pre-school education are inter-linked and interdependent, it follows that they should be grown together and planned together. Taking a strategic view of these services in the round is a major planning challenge. This paper offers guidance on that planning task. It seeks to support those who are involved in planning by identifying relevant information, advising on the processes by which plans should be developed and consulted upon, and setting the context for their implementation. In so doing, this paper aims to help forward the production of integrated plans for childcare and pre-school education in every local authority area by April 1999.

and

> The development and implementation of proposals for expansion of childcare services will depend on a *range of* stakeholders, including the private and

voluntary sectors. The key task in this area will be to identify demand and promote a coordinated response from suppliers of (mainly charged) childcare places. All those with an interest in developing childcare services will face the uncertainty of decisions by parents seeking choice and flexibility and by independent funders which will influence the size and shape of the childcare market. In these circumstances, the 'implementation' of the childcare parts of a plan is bound to involve more monitoring and adjustment than is likely to be the case for pre-school education.

Scottish Office (1998)

In reality, the first and most important aim for the partnership and the local authority was to increase the number of places, ensuring not only the promised total coverage of part time nursery education for four-year-olds but also a massive expansion in full day care places signaled by the National Childcare Strategy.

As Kids' Clubs Network announced:

The National Childcare Strategy will create new childcare places for up to one million children. A new Childcare Tax Credit included in the WFTC will provide parents with help for childcare costs.

Kids' Clubs Network Conference (1999)

This was then quantified using data from the 1999 plans.

Table 2.1 The projected increase in childcare in England 1999–2003

Region	Projected increase in provision by 2003 (%)
North East	525
North West	400
Yorkshire and Humberside	332
East Midlands	543
West Midlands	400
London	217
South West	400
Home Counties	681
South	588
East Anglia	257
Total	**408**

HERA 2, a European-funded joint project on childcare training and qualifications from Suffolk County Council, the National Children's

Bureau and London Guildhall University, reviewed the plans for the Early Years National Training Organisation in order to estimate the future training and qualification needs of the workforce. They came to the conclusion that, if stated targets were met, the plans represented a possible increase in the childcare workforce of 33,000 over the life of the initiative.

The audit requirement

The first step in meeting such massive expansion targets was to ensure that everyone knew what was already in place. The guidance included a requirement to produce a childcare audit for each local authority area prior to the writing of the plan and on which the plan could be based. The audit duty was described as follows:

> Local audits will provide the essential information local partnerships will need to make assessments of shortfalls of supply and demand for childcare and other parent/child support services. In the light of the audit, partnerships will be required to draw up local plans setting priorities for meeting those shortfalls. The information collected will enable partnerships to establish a baseline, against which to monitor progress at local level. It will also provide the basic information and evidence which partnerships will need to secure a share of potential new sources of funding.
>
> *(DfEE, 1998a)*

The guidance went on to detail the information which partnerships were expected to collect in this initial audit and to keep updated in the future. Some suggestions were made about possible sources of information for the statistics and examples given of local authorities which had already worked on similar exercises. Weighting was also given to some parts of the information: essential requirements were in bold text while some additional, discretionary information was put in italics for partnerships to include if they had the capacity to do so. The required information also included consultations with parents, children and young people and employers in order to estimate unmet demand for early years services.

Partnerships were expected to have completed their audit by December 1998 in order for it to inform the writing of the plan, which was due for submission to the DfEE by 1 February 1999. Information which the Early Childhood Unit has obtained from the Local Authority Coordinators' Network indicates that some partnerships began work on aspects of the audit when they received draft guidance in the summer. However, for others, work did not begin until after final guidance was issued, some were still completing audits up to the plan submission deadline and some had still not finished by March.

The DfEE admitted that the audit would be a challenge in some areas and that the deadline was tight:

> We recognise that for many partnerships these local audits may present considerable difficulties as key information concerning predictors of demand, and indicators of supply may not presently be available.
>
> *(DfEE, 1998a)*

However, they invested £12 million in the partnerships' work in this area and they went on to emphasise the importance of the audits:

> Ultimately, the quality of local early years development and childcare partnerships' plans for implementing the National Childcare Strategy will rely heavily on the quality of information collected, and how effectively local partnerships exercise their judgement.
>
> *(DfEE, 1998a)*

This last quotation is key to the process described in this report. The audit was not just an exercise to be completed by a set date and referred to in the plan, it was a tool to be used by members of the partnership in deciding their priorities and the future shape of the service in their local authority area.

The requirements of the plan

The plans represented a massive expansion exercise and the requirements for them were extensive.

To begin with the planning was to have five, overarching principles against which to assess the plans and the services which they were designed to deliver:

- affordability;
- accessibility;
- diversity;
- quality;
- partnership.

The plan itself consisted only of the statement that a free, part time nursery education place would be made available for all four-year-olds whose parents wanted one. All the other plan requirements were to be contained in nine annexes, as follows.

Annex one
Introduction and background to include:
- summary of expenditure;
- information on the partnership;
- how the wishes of parents, children and employers had been taken into account;
- the health of the private and voluntary sectors;
- the effect of local employment and training patterns;
- any additional consultation carried out;
- level of confidence in the audit and Year 2000 compliance.

Annex three
Provision of places for three-year-olds (guidance on this was received later and so partnerships were given a later deadline for this annex), some partnerships were given funding to increase places for three-year-olds in 1999–2000 to 60 per cent coverage, other partnerships were asked to show how this target could be reached in the future.

Annex five
Strategies for recruitment, training and quality to include:
- quality assurance provisions including registration and inspection services;
- plans for improving the quality of provision beyond minimum standards;
- ensuring the quality of educational provision across settings (including registered nursery inspection);
- ways in which a qualified teacher would be involved in all education-funded settings from September 1999;
- a training and recruitment strategy.

Annex seven
Funding to include:
- separate information for the two distinct funding streams of education and childcare payment systems;
- auditing;
- sources of funding;
- an initial bid form;
- a summary of how additional funding within the Revenue Support Grant (RSG) would be allocated;
- how assistance would be provided to the New Opportunities Fund on assessing bids for out-of-school childcare provision.

Annex nine
Additional elements (optional) to include:
- links with neighbouring partnerships;
- local dissemination of good practice;
- innovative ways of integrating childcare and education;
- improvement of parental and family support;
- promotion of family learning;
- promotion of other family support services.

Annex two
Access and admissions to include:
- equal opportunities;
- explanation of the local authority's admissions policy for early years education in the maintained sector.

Annex four
The preparation for and delivery of new places to include:
- local capacity and infrastructure building;
- access to infrastructure support;
- detailed plans for delivering new places with targets for out-of-school childcare places and childcare places for children from birth to age three;
- targets for increasing employer support.

Annex six
Children's information service to include:
- an information strategy;
- assessment of current provision;
- details of planned developments and how these would link in with a projected national information line.

Annex eight
Special educational needs to include:
- the support to be offered to funded early education providers;
- an overview of childcare provision available locally;
- specialist training available;
- information available for parents.

Throughout ran a requirement that all aspects of the plan should refer back to the relevant information within the audit.

This was not only an extensive list, it was also an exercise which required a sophisticated grasp of local circumstances and potential and how these articulated with national aspirations. The final guidance (still without the three-year-olds' duty) was not available until 14 October 1998 and the audit was required to be completed by December so that it could inform a plan to be submitted to the DfEE on 2 February 1999. In addition, during this time a very heterogeneous, new partnership had to be brought together to oversee the process.

The 2000–2001 guidance has been rewritten to include a plan checklist which is designed to meet the following aims in order to:

- make it easier for partnerships to understand what has to be included in the plan and to understand the process of scrutiny;
- allow servicing officers to self-assess on whether or not they have met requirements;
- allow DfEE officials a coherent way to do an initial assessment of plans;
- place statistical tables together in the overall checklist, so that target figures can be seen at a glance.

The checklist follows the sequence of the plan and the audit, which do have to be redone, but there are no changes to the categories which have to be covered. The changes are in the detail which is being required. Examples of where this was lacking in the 1999 plans are funding strategies, because it was felt that very few plans had detailed forward planning in this respect, and equal opportunities strategies, including provision for children with special educational needs.

Conclusion

As we can see, by juxtaposing the list of partnership aims with the list of plan contents, the aims of partnerships are wider than writing plans and meeting targets and not all targets are about numbers of places. Other features from the list of aims are there to:

- ensure that the plan meets the needs of children and parents;
- ensure that the plan enhances the care, play and educational experiences of children up to the age of 14;
- bring together the maintained, private and voluntary sectors in a spirit of cooperation;
- be directed by the diverse needs and aspirations of children and parents locally;

- pay attention to family support;
- be directed by the needs of the local employment situation;
- generate genuine partnership and debate leading to agreement on how such needs can be met.

These are targets which are yet to be given measurable criteria for success. They cluster around issues such as partnership development, the development of consultation mechanisms, the development of quality standards and processes for implementing them, and the connections with local economic development. Missing from this list, but a stated high priority for ministers, is a move towards integrated services which allow children access to care and education in a single setting and which are mirrored by an integrated management, support and funding structure.

The list reads like a Utopian agenda rather than a practical set of tasks for a loose and newly created organisation. However, the aims are all vital if the concept of partnership planning to meet real community needs is to be taken seriously. The big gap in the first year was between the reality of the partnership structures and what they were being asked to do. The gap was filled by frenetic activity on the part of local authority officers who were trying simultaneously to meet the hard targets for places and to develop an infrastructure which would deliver them. There was little time to do partnership development or community consultation and, consequently, the uneven development of the tasks became more marked as time went on. This has led to frustration on the part of partnership members and decline in enthusiasm which, among other things, will be exemplified in the next chapter.

However, as mentioned in the Introduction, partnerships hold the potential to be a new and empowering way of meeting the needs of communities and the children who live in them. They can be forums for critical discussion of the nature of services: where they are, who they serve and what work takes place in them. They can also bring together enough members to ensure coverage of all relevant local initiatives, thus achieving far better liaison and more coordinated planning than has happened in the past. Most importantly, they can do all this on a local level in response to the articulated needs of specific communities, but only if there is space for this within the agenda laid down by central government.

3   Telling it like it is

'The idea of "partnership", which occurs throughout the Children Act, is a complex one. There are many different groups working in partnership. The term partnership itself implies equity, which many parents feel they do not have, particularly when there is a lack of choice either of the type of childcare, or of what happens within their childcare setting. Developments now taking place are beginning to address these complex issues. However, there needs to be continued debate about what partnership means in relation to service users and providers alike. The development of the Early Years Development and Childcare Partnership and Planning framework has facilitated active joint planning with all parties, through working groups and varied planning activities.'

London Borough of Sutton (1999)

In this chapter, we try to outline some of the main issues which have arisen over the past two years as local authorities and their partners have struggled to produce their own 'grand result'. Despite the emphasis by the Government and some national childcare organisations on hard expansion targets, most people have recognised that they are in a way attempting a much wider project, one which Robert Owen would have recognised as comprehending the whole business of life. Bringing disparate groups of people together to debate and plan a common purpose; deciding on that purpose; analysing their current situation and planning for the future; linking with myriad other projects; spending money wisely and accountably; consulting with the community, especially those who have not traditionally been heard; balancing the needs of politicians and bureaucracies with the needs of communities; reporting back faithfully to all stakeholders; and setting up systems and processes to turn this into an ongoing task.

If the Government had simply wanted to create large numbers of new childcare and education places, they could have divided up their admittedly large sums of money between the bureaucracies, in both the statutory and voluntary sector, which already knew how to do this. Instead, they introduced the project of partnership and community auditing and consultation, as a hurried response to the many voices in the early years sector which made themselves heard when the Government failed to bring together a comprehensive policy for the support of the bringing up of children. So how was this process handled in reality? How were so many discordant voices reconciled? This is, of course, a short period of time in which to make any judgements, but judgements are being made and the partnerships are being scored on their performance. It is therefore timely to look at available data, both quantitative and qualitative, to have some idea of how the partnerships perceive their roles and responsibilities and the fitness for purpose of the mechanisms which support them.

Listed in this chapter, in tabled format (see pp. 33–43) are four information sources relating to the early years development and childcare plans and partnerships between May 1997 and September 1999, which were available to the Early Childhood Unit in the course of its work. Whilst these sources were not specifically collected for the purpose of analysis, they are amenable to a form of analysis which at the very least offers a reliable map of the issues within the early years and childcare environment which are most likely to affect the outputs of the partnerships. Each set of information has been systematically collected and is analysed here against a group of themes which have emerged within the myriad discussions at all levels of involvement to which we have been party. The four sets of information are:

- Records of more than forty regional meetings of the Local Authority Early Years Coordinators' Network held between November 1997 and September 1999. Membership of the Network is open to all local authority coordinators, partnership servicing officers, heads of service and other key posts. These are the people who for the most part have been responsible for setting up their partnerships, writing the plans and running the services within their respective authorities. Also included in this set of information are the records of the eight national meetings of the Network and, more recently, of the Network's meeting with the Minister, Margaret Hodge, on 21 June 1999. It is worth noting that almost every local authority in England has been involved at one time or another and we have had presentations and discussion with our colleagues in Northern Ireland, Wales and Scotland.
- Documentation from the Early Childhood Unit Childcare Audit Partnership Project which involved five local authorities and the following national partners: National Childminding Association, Department of Applied Social Studies and Social Research, University of Oxford, and Working for Childcare. Essentially, this was a mentoring scheme to assist local project teams to make sense of the audit requirement.

- Information drawn from individual consultancies, conferences and partnership development days undertaken by the Early Childhood Unit.
- Information from the analysis of 118 EYDCP undertaken by the HERA 2 project, of which ECU is a partner, on behalf of the National Training Organisation and NCMA.

In interrogating this information, we identified 23 themes or areas as being of importance:

- the status, resourcing and organisational structure of the local authority project team involved in this work;
- the extent to which there was a vision for the project including shared, articulated aspirations for children;
- the degree and form of consultation and participation;
- the extent modernisation of local government was on the agenda;
- the extent to which the audit was used as a planning tool;
- the existence of a hierarchy of planning within the local authorities, for example, what status did the EYDCP have in relation to the Education Plan or the Children's Services Plan?
- the approach to professional integration;
- the existence of compartmentalisation or territoriality;
- processes for accountability, responsibility and decision-making;
- the approach to the integration of care and education;
- the approach to issues of recruitment and retention of staff;
- the approach to quality and equality;
- the approach to target-setting;
- the approach to training;
- the effect of the deadlines;
- approaches to providing children's information services;
- targeting disadvantage;
- the existence of a methodology for expansion;
- the approach to sustainability;
- the approach to capacity-building;
- the approach to costing;
- provision for children with special needs;
- the relationship to central government.

We looked for evidence on these issues from each of our sources and have drawn conclusions about the process of partnership planning over this period. Our sources are shown in table form with examples of evidence provided by each under the 23 identified topics. (See glossary on page 41 for abbreviations.)

Table 3.1 Process of partnership planning

	Local Authority Early Years Coordinators Network	Consultancy and development work	Early Childhood Unit Childcare Audit Partnership project	HERA 2 Early Years Development and Childcare Plan Audit
Status and resourcing of LA Project Team, organisation and structures	Within the network there is evidence of huge variation in levels and scope of organisation. A growing number have well-resourced integrated services with permanent staff and strategic planning responsibilities. (Although none are the same.) Some are new unitary authorities who brought together seconded staff at very short notice. In many instances single post-holders were servicing the plans, partnerships and audits. There is significant variation in job descriptions, titles and responsibilities. Most lead posts are in education services but by no means all. Few of the heads of service posts are graded at equivalent levels with assistant director posts in either social services or education. Very varied pay scales and one example of a post-holder being downgraded while in post. Difficulty of accessing RSG amounts by this group because not in positions of power.	**Difficulties with joint working:** Partnership officers in education and/or early years joint appointments lacking support from social services or no lead within the authority to ensure successful joint work on initiatives. **Lack of status of posts:** One authority was seeking to give the partnership extensive responsibilities but the LA project team seemed to be under-resourced. In one London borough there were very genuine efforts being made to give the partnership a definite decision-making role. However the capacity of the LA to facilitate this was compromised because there were so few senior managers and they had huge workloads. In another authority there were very serious efforts to be transparent and to differentiate the complementary roles of the partnership and the LA but again, latter seemed to be compromised by insufficient numbers of servicing staff.	**NU:** New officer appointed at fairly low level but with good joint line management from two departments. However, decisions were sometimes slow and their own priorities had to take precedence, for example Quality Protects. A clerk was given job of doing audit and had trouble getting the support she needed from other departments. **C:** Extra officer seconded to pull project together with help of existing audit officer - but went on sick leave. Integrated team was being established at the same time and elected members were unhappy about the work required and often overruled partnership decisions. **NU:** Only rudimentary development of a project team. Team consisted of two people with administrative back-up, and an additional person brought in to work on the purchased GIS package. However, the senior officer had equally demanding responsibilities in other areas of the LEA and could not work full time on the early years aspects. Plans were made to set up an enabling team which was to be corporately resourced. Once appointed, it was to include the development workers.	

	Local Authority Early Years Coordinators Network	Consultancy and development work	Early Childhood Unit Childcare Audit Partnership project	HERA 2 Early Years Development and Childcare Plan Audit
Vision including shared articulated aspirations for children	In many instances servicing staff report real difficulties in establishing and maintaining a guiding vision. This is crucially affected by the capacity for partnership development. Little spare time for this, but central to building and negotiating a vision'.	**NU:** Used the UN Convention as their vision probably because of a pre-existing alliance within the voluntary sector.	**NU:** The authority had a holistic regeneration strategy but had not formulated a vision for children's services. There was not an articulated plan to integrate services although there was a lead from social services to build a preventive infrastructure in the Children's Services Plan. **NU:** Here the LEA were in the position of having excellent SATs results and an extremely good family learning service. However there was little in the way of any integrated expression of shared aspirations for children.	Little evidence of links with other key initiatives such as Quality Protects or HAZ and EAZs.
Consultation participation	Coordinators report diverse approaches to consultation. It is striking, however, that in most instances they have felt that specific consultation needed to be undertaken for their childcare audit rather than drawing on existing work with children, parents and employers. Very few reported that these arrangements were ongoing.	**NU:** Had run into some difficulty with their audit but had separately done an audit of networks within each of their childcare planning areas (their geographical unit) and constructed their partnership process to systematically take account of these. **C:** Good consultation on the childcare needs of older children with clear conclusions to guide practice about what features young people would like in services.	**NU:** Had little in the way of consultation but became very enthusiastic about direct consultation with children and planned to have a parents' college of representatives to get the views of parents directly into the partnership. They also successfully became a Sure Start Trailblazer and undertook direct consultation with the chosen community with vigour.	

	Local Authority Early Years Coordinators Network	Consultancy and development work	Early Childhood Unit Childcare Audit Partnership project	HERA 2 Early Years Development and Childcare Plan Audit
Modernisation	Most of the coordinators saw themselves on the fringes of this with some notable exceptions. There is also evidence of restructuring taking place in response to budget reductions in a significant number of authorities especially in the London boroughs.	In one authority, plans for the new committee structure had marginalised the partnership by showing a connecting line to partnerships and other quangos'.	**NU:** To a certain extent the modernisation agenda had been part of the backdrop to the ways in which the authority had been set up. However, their community consultation structure was not evident and neither were the scrutiny structures. **NU:** Some restructuring was evident at the level of first-tier officers but plans for locality committees were not agreed. There was no obvious steer to link the early years &üchildcare planning to other systems. **LB:** This authority had chosen early years as a Best Value pilot and had spent much time working on fitting the criteria.	
Use of audit as planning tool	Many authorities had brought in external consultants to do the audit for them with varying degrees of satisfaction. What was striking was that in most instances irrespective of who had done the audit it had been done as a one off exercise. Most did not have adequate electronically assisted systems to link the audit to other audits in the authority and beyond, for example crime reduction audits, nor to the registration and inspection systems.	**NU:** Had clearly used the audit to prioritise activity and had done a separate audit of networks. The geographical unit used was specially designated childcare areas. **C:** Still has no GIS system in place well into 1999 and is anticipating difficulties in harmonising systems.	**NU:** Combined the childcare audit with their regeneration plan which spans the whole borough to good effect mapping their post coded data within the identified regeneration areas. **NU:** Used postcoded data, mapping within their ward boundaries. Comprehensive and very easy to use data offering comparisons. Locally gathered qualitative data was then available to both the partnership and the officers of the local authority. Audit was set up on database.	Quantitative data was presented differently by many partnerships and not all provided data in all the categories.

	Local Authority Early Years Coordinators Network	Consultancy and development work	Early Childhood Unit Childcare Audit Partnership project	HERA 2 Early Years Development and Childcare Plan Audit
Planning hierarchy, admissions	Many authorities reported that Education Development Plans were taking precedence both in terms of resources put in to undertake the work and for decision making. There was little clarity anywhere about the relationship expected by DfEE between EDPs and the EYDCPs. The links with the CSPs seemed shaky.	**NU:** Quality Protects agenda and Education Development Plan took a high profile just as plan was being written. This affected the senior manager's ability to give detailed support to staff - resulting in some changes being made to the Plan very late in the day.	**NU:** There was a feeling that the Education Development Plan had taken precedence and that there were few links to the Children's Services Plan. Admissions caused conflict but there was no real resolution of this. **NU:** Candid acknowledgement that the Education Development Plan had precedence. Active working relationship with SSD but unresolved issues regarding overlap between Children's Services Plans and EYDCPs.	
Approach to professional integration	Most authorities were not advanced in this respect.		**NU:** High achieving education authority with highly developed teaching outreach methodologies which were collaborative but with no overarching approach to professional integration.	
Compart- mentalism, department- alism, terri- toriality	Most authorities reported that at least people from different departments were sitting down talking to each other clearly seeing this as progress.		**NU:** Education were a distinct grouping but Planning were very cooperative. Early years childcare still seemed to be on the fringes of economic development. **NU:** New unitary with no separatist traditions. **NU:** Two departments located in same building made for easier liaison. Willingness to be cooperative, and joint managers worked very effectively. Pleasant personalities made an enormous difference despite heavy workloads.	

	Local Authority Early Years Coordinators Network	Consultancy and development work	Early Childhood Unit Childcare Audit Partnership project	HERA 2 Early Years Development and Childcare Plan Audit
Accountability Responsibility Decision-making	Many authorities struggled to be clear in their lines of accountability. This was raised by the coordinators as a serious issue with the Minister on 21.6.99. It seemed that the better resourced and thought through the authority was in terms of its vision. The better the differentiation on accountability and decision-making. Coordinators were prepared to share complex decisions and information within their partnerships.	**One new unitary council** actively sought to find ways of dealing with the lack of clarity between the roles of the partnership and the LA.	**NU:** Feeling of real openness in the partnership; decision-making beyond partnership level was less clear. First tier officers seemed remote. **NU:** Could seem idiosyncratic and/or contradictory. LA seemed to make decisions in isolation and there was no clear idea of what the partnership could or could not do.	
Model of integrating services, Approach to diversity	The overwhelming majority of authorities do not have a model for integration which is part of a strategy for expansion. Rather, many of them have thought about or done an Early Excellence bid as one-off exercise only. However, there is evidence of intended strategic roll-out in some places. It is not yet clear how authorities are viewing Sure Start as an integrated model.	**C:** Produced a network of networks model which linked to both a regeneration partnership and education action zone, using childminders to ensure continuity of experience for the children.	**NU:** Decided to consider a locality network model and based the strategy for expansion on this. There were no established forums of private and voluntary sector providers. However, a diverse partnership was quickly established for Sure Start. **NU:** as above, but lack if clarity on the ownership of this proposal. There was little established informal networks outside the maintained sector.	Eight partnerships mentioned creating a coordinator post to oversee the plan but few mentioned the development of an integrated service as a whole.
Recruitment and retention of staff	All of the coordinators were concerned about this and raised it with the Minister on 21.6.99. Many reported problems in recruiting appropriately skilled development workers and that authorities tended to re-evaluate pay scales downwards. One metropolitan authority with a long established integrated service had committed to three-year development posts. This has not been possible for many others.	**NU:** Targeted a childminding network as an opportunity to recruit new workers and develop retention strategies for existing minders.	**NU:** Has created a specific strategy for targeting potential new workers via colleges and employment schemes and setting up specific induction for them.	11 partnerships mentioned developing induction courses for workforce as a whole. This will need to link with the national orientation course.

	Local Authority Early Years Coordinators Network	Consultancy and development work	Early Childhood Unit Childcare Audit Partnership project	HERA 2 Early Years Development and Childcare Plan Audit
Approach to equality and quality	It has been our impression that coordinators have not had time to think through what is happening in this area.	One county partnership officer expressed the particular problems of mainly white' areas but there is no strategy on this to date.	**NU:** Systematic approach to inclusion for children with SEN and rigorous efforts to consult with such children. 18 primary schools linked to family learning groups were kite marked.	Only four partnerships noted a lack of provision for children from minority ethnic groups or the need to recruit staff from these groups
Approach to target setting	Many reported that problems were beginning to emerge in areas of serious disadvantage in that partnership members often expressed the view that areas could be eligible for too many grants. Some seem reluctant to target disadvantage as heavily as the statistics suggest is warranted.		**NU:** Calculated on the basis of what seemed feasible within their priorities. Linked development workers to localities and thereby linked targets to need at the local level. **NU:** Attempted to use a locality model setting targets against need and the previous record of the out of school funding initiative, but this caused some conflict.	Emphasis noted on OOS places and on the development of childminding (including networks). Not all partnerships set targets across the board - many mentioned only one or two areas of provision in terms of actual figures.
Training	There is concern about the scale of training needed to support the expansion targets which central government wish to see. Great interest in the national framework but concern that progress seems delayed and that this will affect local developments.	Work on the ECU's Working in Partnership development programme has shown the importance of addressing the training needs of partnership members and development workers. This should link with an overall training strategy.	**NU:** Collaborative training plan but not strategically linked to employment.	Half the partnerships mentioned low levels of qualifications, particularly for OOS workers and childminders. Only 18% of partnerships set qualification targets for their workforce. Most listed the training needs of the workforce, but there seems to be no standard methodology for this assessment. Some new areas were mentioned which aren't reflected in the National Occupational Standards. 70% had started to develop training strategies but these varied considerably, most included locally developed courses.

	Local Authority Early Years Coordinators Network	Consultancy and development work	Early Childhood Unit Childcare Audit Partnership project	HERA 2 Early Years Development and Childcare Plan Audit
Deadlines	Deadlines had been met but at a cost. There is anecdotal evidence of increases in stress-related sickness and some feeling that time spent in preparing the plans and graining agreement to them has risked stifling pre-existing development of more long term value. Most audits were not completed in time to fully inform the plans. One was not launched until mid-1999.	**C:** One audit officer was unable to finish due to sick leave. **NU:** Partnership officer left on long-term, stress-related sick leave.	**NU:** Able to meet deadlines because a few staff prepared to work all hours. **NU:** Able to work all hours. Last minute disagreements caused delays and additional stress. Staff on sick leave with stress-related conditions.	
Childcare Information Service	Many coordinators report that they are struggling with this. Systems have not been as straightforward to put in place as they had been led to believe and deadlines are slipping. In one region, an existing CIS has been able to offer a service on contract to a number of partnerships.	**C:** After six years of discussions, a database is still not agreed, nor a GIS. There is now difficultly in dovetailing all of the necessary developments.	**NU:** Worked within a small network of surrounding authorities to initiate a system. However, no coherent links yet to other systems. Some existing local information services were not well used and there was some poor cooperation with the local authorities. This meant negotiation was needed to implement change.	
Targeting disadvantage	See Approach to target setting'. Some local concern over areas which are the target for multiple programmes of funding. Coordinators have been sharing information regionally on the use of criteria, for example for targeting the three-year-old funding.	**C:** Very clear areas of both urban and rural disadvantage shown by audit and targeted for specific projects, for example childminding networks. Rural disadvantage has proved hard to target within current funding schemes.	**NU:** Systematic comparisons were made throughout the audit between need and planned services.	Childminding networks were being developed in many authorities, often targeting specific groups including minority ethnic groups, children with special needs and, most often, children in need.

	Local Authority Early Years Coordinators Network	Consultancy and development work	Early Childhood Unit Childcare Audit Partnership project	HERA 2 Early Years Development and Childcare Plan Audit
Expansion methodology	Most people appear not to have such a methodology, rather targets have been developed in a piecemeal and sometimes arbitrary way.	Two counties have used an existing network of local forums as the basis for a locality network feeding into the main partnership. Another has appointed facilitators for local partnerships and will provide them with an information and practice guide.	**NU:** Locality based networks corresponding to identified need and linked to development workers. **NU:** Same model as above but this subsequently became disputed. **NU2:** Uses same model but with larger areas and groups based on existing forum structure.	Majority of partnerships mentioned using childminding networks to expand provision.
Approach to sustainability	This is almost universally thought to be a big issue. The WFTC is being welcomed but there is little clarity how this will sustain places in the most disadvantaged areas. Sustainability is not being linked to capacity building sufficiently. Some authorities felt that there had been considerable development in OOS provision in the previous year and that these more viable groups needed support to continue. Workers should not be used to set up new groups in less viable areas.	**C:** Childminding Network model will use attachment to existing groups to ensure long-term viability and support and to reduce network costs.	**NU:** Closely linked to capacity building, lifelong learning and the need to increase skills and self confidence. Looking to Sure Start trailblazer as exemplar. **NU:** Initially sought to have a capacity building, community development approach but this became conflicted as they struggled with divisions between the sectors and departments. **NU:** Considered by existing OOS development workers to be a big problem. Revised initial targets downwards to reflect this.	Many partnerships were establishing a sustainability fund to support failing provision and ensure their viability.
Approach to capacity building	Capacity building is often confused with infrastructure development. It is not as yet clear how most partnerships are differentiating and approaching this. New coordinator posts have been created to oversee developments.		The project worked on a Community partnership model of capacity building which is now being developed in most of the authorities (see Appendix 1).	Varied approaches but most included development officers appointed by the LA with local forums as their network. There is evidence that the developmental emphasis has shifted from the voluntary sector to the LA even for the development of childminding networks. Childminder recruitment was key to capacity building in many plans but this could be difficult as childminder numbers are declining.

	Local Authority Early Years Coordinators Network	Consultancy and development work	Early Childhood Unit Childcare Audit Partnership project	HERA 2 Early Years Development and Childcare Plan Audit
Approach to costing	There is little in the way of a unified approach to costing. Most people do not use devices such as cost trees.		**NU:** Aware of cost tree methodology but did not apply it.	
Special needs	Coordinators welcome the additional emphasis given to special needs. Many queries about how this can be funded given standard unit costings.		**NU:** Considerable understanding linked through head of service who was an educational psychologist.	Childminder networks specifically targeted for this in some plans.
Relationship to central government	Generally thought not to be as good as it should be. Coordinators do not feel that they are a first source for consultation with central government and that they should have a systematic dialogue. Most authorities believe that the designation of accepted' or deferred' for their plans was done inconsistently and that there has been no meaningful feedback from DfEE on this. They feel there are jobs only central government can do, for example liaison with planners and Customs and Excise over VAT, and with material information sources for the audit.		There were very variable experiences. **NU:** Identified in first tranche of three-year-old money and for Sure Start and Plan accepted unconditionally. They had been prepared to lobby via MPs. **NU:** Did not get three-year-old money and was not identified for first round of Sure Start. It was believed Plan only received conditional approval because of complaints from the private sector.	

Abbreviations used in the table
C - county council; CSP - Children's Services Plan; EAZ - Education Action Zone; EDP - Education Development Plan; EYDCP - Early Years Development and Childcare Plan; GIS - Geographical Information System; HAZ - Health Action Zone; LA - local authority; LB - London borough; LEA - local education authority; NU - new unitary council; OOS - out-of-school; RSG - Revenue Support Grant; SAT - Standard Assessment Test; WFTC - Working Families' Tax Credit.

Emergent issues

Success

First of all, it is overwhelmingly the case that the early years and childcare sector has responded to the tasks set by central government with almost slavish determination and enormous energy. In the main, the workforce has been made up of dedicated women who have been banging the drum for their sector for many years. Given the initial state of play and level of funding, it is a very significant achievement that all plans have been submitted more-or-less on time and that many places have also submitted Early Excellence and Sure Start proposals.

What this means is that there is a plan and an audit of sorts in every authority in the country and, probably for the first time, many of them are adopting a common methodology which includes community development and a strategic approach to the promotion of social inclusion and expansion of places. If central government wishes to drive through its policies on a systematic and equitable basis, then it is certainly true that the basic mechanisms are in place. What a start! What follows is a listing of the issues which will need to be considered to some extent, if this initial success is to be built on.

Local authority structures

The efficacy of the local project teams which worked with the ECU on audits and partnership development was a significant factor. It is frequently pointed out that existing local authority management structures are ill-equipped to deal with partnership working, private/public initiatives and mixed economies of service delivery and funding. The Best Value and modernisation agenda was designed partly to deal with this. However, the patchwork of services has forced flexibility onto local authorities in the area of early education and childcare over the last 15 years, hence the creation of integrated and coordinated units to manage these services within some local authorities, such as Manchester, Kirklees and Southwark. However, these units initially often worked in hostile environments and had to struggle to capture and control their own budgets. With the range of new early years initiatives and the significant funding which accompanies them, these services have attained a higher profile both on a national and local level. This has not always been matched by equal recognition within local authorities, where their development and status has often lagged behind their national significance. The fact that nursery education for four-year-olds was the first element of this significant funding was one factor which has led to the integration of management within education departments.

However, the precedent for this had already been set by those early integrated units which were almost all in education. This was mirrored in 1998 by the movement of early years services into the DfEE at national level.

Problems still exist, however, as the traditional lack of status attached to these services led to a significant under-management of them within local authorities when the new initiatives arrived. Often, all the work of creating partnerships, developing them, doing the audit and writing the plan fell to one or two people who had been employed in a very different role. In some authorities there was no-one in such a role and people had to be seconded or moved at short notice and on short-term contracts with very little idea of what the job would involve. Line management was difficult in such a situation, as line managers also might have had little idea what was involved or might have been sharing the line management function with people in other departments. This latter arrangement, often entered into in order not to tread on toes, could be disastrous for the workers being managed unless good working relationships already existed between these people. However, this is unlikely, given the reason for the arrangement! The examples which we know of where it did work appear to have been because of the personalities involved. Is this an exception which proves the rule?

Coordinators also gave information about the varied pay scales being used for the same job, as well as attempts at downgrading the posts. Obviously, gradings will reflect real differences in job descriptions, but the question remains as to why there are such big differences. In part, the lack of coherence reflects the hybrid nature of many of these posts and, as a result, it is perhaps important to begin to argue for the delineation of a new professional grouping with its own qualifications and pay structure. Equally important here will be the acceptance of how care, play and education are all interconnected.

Additionally, the patchwork of services was often now being coordinated by a local authority department which usually has very little experience of working with the voluntary and private sectors, no knowledge of the legislation by which they are regulated and little understanding of their history or rationale. This has had obvious repercussions in the debate about the role of playgroups and the possibility of maintaining a mixed economy of provision in the face of central government funding for three- and four-year-olds and is also immensely important in the discussions around the quality standards which partnerships are expected to equalise across all sectors of provision. The management of this sector by the local education authority (LEA), reinforced by the requirements in the plan guidance for qualified teacher input into funded settings, has usually meant that LEA primary or nursery inspectors and advisory teachers have been given responsibility for this area. This is a development which has not always been popular with the providers themselves, their own professional associations or those who previously supported them from within social services inspection units. Even where this has not proved a problem, there are implications for the type of standards which will be set by support staff without a background in child day care and this needs to be an area of discussion and resolution by partnerships.

This also relates to the local authority's vision for the service. Those authorities which already had a well-developed policy in this area, which meant that they had coordination or integration in place and a realistic staffing structure with the budget to support it, were the ones most likely to be able to run with the new developments and get the most out of them. This was a conclusion which also arose from the ECU's study of the voucher scheme (Owen and McQuail, 1998) and from the ongoing reviews of the Audit Commission and the District Audit.

The HERA 2 survey also noted that, although a lot of partnerships referred to the need to establish an integrated service as part of their infrastructure developments, very few mentioned other areas with which there are obvious connections, such as health and education action zones or Single Regeneration Budget bids.

Time

Everyone has repeatedly said that the timescales are absurdly short and, as already mentioned, it is to the great credit of the coordinators and partnership officers that they have met these deadlines. It is not clear, however, what the cost has been. Evidence from the Coordinators' Network is that aims and objectives which could have been pursued at local level with some coherence have of necessity been neglected, whilst the imposed targets for new places have been prioritised. Without routine monitoring, it will be impossible to see what the actual impact of this will be. Existing DfEE-sponsored research and national development projects seem to be weighted towards assessing success in achieving the centrally-imposed targets, rather than success in laying down the developmental foundations. Time for reflection and assessment is all too often lacking in good practice in direct work with children and it is therefore vital that the delivery of new policy is seen to be considered, well judged and seriously reflected on, so that a whole generation of children are not at the mercy of ideology. As Dahlberg, Moss and Pence have recently said:

> We live in a world that is increasingly time-governed, driven by new technologies and demands for increasing productivity. We are saturated with

information. We demand and expect instant answers and quick fixes. We do not make time for other things, not least reflection, dialogue, critical thinking, working the tensions between theory and practice.

G Dahlberg, P Moss and A Pence (1999) p. 17

The guidance and the assessment of plans

This was, and is, a massive expansion exercise for a sector which ranged in scope from local authorities with integrated multi-million pound budgets to those where most groups raised their funds from jumble sales. Additionally, the DfEE laid down very tight timetables for planning, monitoring and delivering places in order to ensure some financial accountability for the unprecedented public funding which was flowing into the sector. For example, every partnership must submit a quarterly return indicating their progress in meeting targets for the expansion of places.

However, the first round of EYDCPs showed enormous variability. The HERA 2 report referred to above came to the following conclusion:

> Finally, there is little consistency in the way in which plans are written and presented, and in many cases, data presented by partnerships was inconsistent between sections in the plans. For future research purposes, and in order to identify national trends, it might be helpful to give more detailed guidance on presentation of quantitative and qualitative data in the plans.
>
> *C Cordeaux and others (1999)*

The scrutiny put in place by the DfEE after plan submission resulted in an announcement by the Minister in April 1999 to the effect that 102 plans had gained full approval while 48 had gained only deferred approval. This announcement was made at a high-profile conference without the results being given to partnerships or servicing officers beforehand. Indeed, no full report on it has appeared since. The whole exercise came in for a good deal of criticism from those who were being marked in this way. Comments collected from the regional meetings of the Early Years Coordinators' Network and from the partnerships in the ECU's Partnership/Audit Project included the following:

- A feeling that central government wished to make an example of a percentage of partnerships in order to appear to be taking a tough line on standards, without actually jeopardising their own targets by failing anyone outright.
- A number of partnerships had been told that their plans did not require much remedial work by DfEE officials. However, this could

have led to some of the plans, which were initially the poorest, being given full approval after extensive work while the better ones ended up receiving only deferred approval.

- Many examples were given of a failure of communication between partnerships and the DfEE officials, with partnerships being misinformed about potential problems in their plans.
- Complaints were made about the use by the DfEE of short-term, contract staff with little knowledge of the sector and consequent mistakes being made about plan evaluations.
- There was little clarity over the administration of the exercise for those with deferred plans, for example, could they assume that developments could go ahead and be funded pending their rewrite of the plan? It was crucial to know this, given the short timetable for implementation in the first year.

Geography

Each of the EYDC partnerships should be able to rely upon a proper audit of both quantitative and qualitative data, used intelligently by both planners and practitioners to guide priorities and shape decision-making. But the starting points are so unequal and the tasks so disparate. Northern Ireland has an intricate and highly devolved system of partnerships extending across the entire country, built up over seven years since 1992, but is the same size as some of our large counties. In the same way, shire counties sharing jurisdiction with district councils sit side by side with big metropolitan authorities who do not. Then there are the London boroughs with small areas, but huge and transient populations, while other unitary authorities may have populations of little more than 100,000.

It is clearly not sensible to suggest that the planning task is the same in each instance. Quite apart from issues of geography and population, so much depends on the ways in which the early years and childcare agenda has been managed in the past, on the age and history of each authority and how it is responding to the modernisation agenda for local government. In turn, these factors will link to the neighbourhood agendas of the people who need services and to the national agenda for change. Tackling the task of partnership development, auditing and plan writing last year were some authorities that had only been in existence for a few months and the table above shows the very particular problems which they faced. What does it tell us about central government that it has not set as a key priority the identification and implementation of structures which help people to deal with such complexity? Our evidence suggests that prescriptive guidance on target setting and plan writing has served to obscure rather than to illuminate the context within which the planning is taking place. These tricky hurdles allow a 'naming and shaming' exercise to take place, but they will not help partnerships to get it right for the future. Or can it be the case that they are posting out the money and crossing their fingers for satisfactory outcomes?

The audit

The original aim of the ECU's Audit/Partnership Project was to attempt to create a methodology and strategy for the audit and a way of linking it into both partnership development and writing the plan. The sharing of information within the development group undoubtedly contributed to this process and clarified a number of mechanisms and approaches. However, it quickly became clear, and was re-emphasised by the wider coordinators' group, that there were major stumbling blocks to overall coherence. The more obvious stumbling blocks drawn from the above evidence were:

- lack of status and influence of officers when trying to involve other departments;
- lack of available staff with both early years and IT skills;
- lack of systems sophisticated enough to undertake the exercise;
- lack of preliminary discussions by the partnership on their vision for the audit;
- lack of time to complete the audit and consider it before writing the plan (no-one seemed to have done this);
- a tendency to see the audit as a number of discrete exercises rather than a coherent whole (some partnerships hired a number of different external consultants to do these separate parts);
- the use of out-of-date data sets.

The audit should have been interwoven with the whole process of plan and partnership development and, to work most effectively, should have been fully integrated with other audit processes and statistical data collection taking place in the local authority, but this only happened in a few authorities.

The 2000–2001 guidance stipulates that the audit needs to be reworked, even though new categories have not been added to it. Disappointingly, the need for integration with other planning tools and practical suggestions for how this could be effected have not been included, even though examples of this type of work existed in some partnerships and plans in 1999. For more information on the database approach utilised in the Project, see Appendix 1.

Aspiration

What does emerge clearly from all our conversations is how much people want to do well by the children for whom they are responsible. Unlike other sectors, early years and childcare has been a poor relation, something of a backwater for the ambitious. There is a sincerity and depth of experience in these coordinators and others, who have had to fight for years to keep their jobs and their funding, which central government would do well to trust.

Time and again, we find that the services which shine, and there are many, are those who are reaching for something which is better than the status quo. They are also the services who, like Robert Owen, are not to be limited by their targets but have been prepared to see the big picture. They have allowed their targets to arise from the big picture, making connections and coming up with new answers. But those who have not yet been able to do this, and there were many examples where the partnerships had not even articulated a basic set of aspirations for their area, alert us to the fact that there is little in the present heated rush which will encourage this kind of careful and purposeful approach.

Managing change

For many authorities, the new environment requires a fundamental shift in attitude which cannot take place in the space of a few months. As we have pointed out above, and in the table of information sources on pp.33–43, many of the project teams set up to manage the work in the local authorities contained officers who were new, on short-term posts or secondments or had low status and resourcing. As a result, they were not in a position to tackle such fundamental shifts or the blockages which could easily occur in other organisations or departments.

We said above that central government did not deal with this complication by drawing the attention of others to the importance and complexity of the work and an example of this is the many different ways in which communication was handled. Some papers went to local authority officers, some to partnership chairs, some to both, some to directors of education and a few (prompted by the Local Government Association) went to elected members. Chief executives, who should be expected to be in charge, did not receive a communication alerting them to the implications of this work until after the plans had been written, when they alone were sent the letters requesting that the partnerships revise their targets upwards. It could be argued that chief executives should have taken a corporate grip on this work very early on, but this is to ignore the realities of working in a local authority. In some cases, the partnerships just became new battle grounds for old struggles. The DfEE distanced itself from this situation and from what were seen as purely local authority issues, such as the low status of partnership officers and the difficulty of excavating the money allocated via the Revenue Support Grant, but such issues are crucial to the success or failure of the project. They are well-known stumbling blocks and could therefore have been anticipated and allowed for.

Many of the coordinators want to map out the milestones, which will enable them to take stock of what is or is not happening within their partnerships and services, and to assess the real changes in culture which are being made possible. However, the system of quarterly review for the DfEE does not allow for this and most coordinators will not be able to find the time outside of it. Without persistent review of this sort, the partnerships may be hostage to fortune: praised only if they make their targets, damned if they don't.

Sustainability

Almost every partnership has voiced concern about sustainability and their fears are well founded. Consistent evidence from the Out-of-School Funding Initiative has shown that pump-priming a service only works in specific conditions and that there are real difficulties in expecting long-term viability without subsidy. This is especially true in those disadvantaged areas where the market would not naturally produce early years provision or where the Government would like to see economic stimulation and where, for these reasons, much of the funding is targeted.

The Government's decision to allocate funding via the New Opportunities Fund of the National Lottery (NOF) came in for a great deal of criticism from the groups we consulted. There are very specific accountability constraints on this form of public funding and, additionally, a new unit and new systems had to be set up for this area of work. All this has resulted in slow decision-making which is not synchronous with the development timetables of partnerships and which does not allow much flexibility for groups in which sustainability will be a problem. NOF has listened to feedback from partnerships and will doubtless do what it can. A more interesting question is why central government should have chosen to fund such a vital area of development in a way which was bound to make it difficult to reach targets effectively and to sustain places over the long term.

To some extent, the issue of sustainability has been tackled by the implementation of the most generous scheme of assistance for childcare which this country has ever seen: the Working Families' Tax Credit. But the childcare market is highly complex, with individual parents exercising very sophisticated choices in how they make the best balance between work and family. This is just as true for poor parents as for rich parents. Managing supply and demand will therefore be especially complicated in this sector and one of the most important tasks which the new structures will have to tackle.

Community partnership and consultation

Evidence from all sides tells us that many of the above issues can only be tackled by means of systematic community involvement and not by means of hurried one-off bits of consultation. In the long term, the most sustainable forms of childcare will be those which are best melded with local aspirations and ways of bringing up children. The more sophisticated consultation exercises began to offer up valuable information for this type of exercise, for instance, the childcare preferences of children over the age of 12. However, we would argue that this can only be fruitful within an ongoing strategy of community partnership which allows the EYDC partnership to be informed by continuous debate, design, assessment and change at the neighbourhood level. This type of feeding up from local level was recognised in the guidance and taken on board by most partnerships, but our evidence shows that its development has been put off in many areas, due to pressure of work. The local development workers who would have the job of nurturing such partnerships will be engaged almost exclusively in direct support of providers to meet targets at least for the next two years, by which time that provision could well be out of alignment with the needs of the neighbourhood. A few local authorities, possibly those who have a history of early years planning and some resources of their own, may be able to support the partnerships by splitting off this function and ensuring that the work gets done simultaneously.

Appendix 3 outlines some examples of consultation/participation strategies which were put in place by partnerships taking part in the ECU Audit/Partnership Project.

Children and quality

Probably the most commonly expressed issue relates directly to the quality of experience which will actually be achieved for children. It is no exaggeration to say that there is huge concern about what might be happening. The existing patchwork of services is of variable quality and there are very considerable deficits in the availability of appropriately trained, far less experienced, staff. As the Minister, Margaret Hodge, herself has said on numerous occasions, quality is heavily reliant on well-trained and committed staff. The Coordinators' Network has often pointed out that the push to achieve targets, although understandable if the DfEE is to continue to receive Treasury support, could paradoxically result in worse outcomes in terms of children's educational standards and their predisposition to learn.

Nationally, the development of the training and qualifications framework and the establishment of national training organisations for early years and play begins to tackle the fact that early years childcare and education are not attractive careers for the well educated, but it does not address the issue of pay. Government employment schemes such as the New Deal and national traineeships are also focusing on the need to pump more workers into the field, but there are concerns about the motivation and ability of those who come through such schemes and about the ability of existing employers to support their development. Few plans had serious strategies to tackle this area and the DfEE has picked this up in their new guidance, listing eight areas under which the partnership's policy and strategy needs to be detailed. A separate section requires details of the plan to ensure adequate training and in-service development for existing workers. Some partnerships show evidence of beginning to think about this in terms of a more targeted and local identification of potential workers and their support needs and one or two projects now in development might offer valuable examples.

The issue of integrated practice also got rather lost during the flurry of the first plans, but the DfEE stresses that it is still high among ministers' priorities.

> Let there be no doubt that our aim is a comprehensive and integrated approach to good quality early years education and childcare.
> *Estelle Morris, Foreword to* Early Years Development Partnerships and Plans *(DfEE, 1997)*

Despite this, the first 1999–2000 guidance did not include integration in its list of targets and it did not appear as a specific aim of the partnerships. It appeared in the guiding principles as one sentence only under accessibility, 'Provision should include the integration of early years education with childcare' (DfEE, 1998a).

Of course, the Early Excellence Centre initiative was designed specifically to provide examples of good practice in the integration of childcare and education but, again, there has been little to link this initiative strategically with the work of partnerships. Our evidence has shown that, in many areas, bids for EEC status have been submitted in isolation from partnership work, as indeed have Sure Start bids. This is mentioned in the new guidance which asks for a partnership policy, details on how Early Excellence Centres will disseminate good practice and information on other approaches to integration. However, for a society which has historically had a very rigid split between care and education, this is a big conceptual leap and a huge practical task which will require much thought and commitment on the part of partnerships.

The ECU's project, Integration in Practice (1999–2000), funded by the DfEE, is designed to offer partnerships the opportunity and space to have such discussions within the context of the learning support which they are already providing. This will be reported on fully in Spring 2000 and will form the subject of the Year 2000 conference run jointly by NCB and Nottingham Educational Supplies. An interesting initial finding from this project is the strong statutory education bias which has been evident in the contributions to date. Although integration is supposed to be about harmonising care and early education, for all age groups and across all sectors, overwhelmingly, those attending the project seminars have been local authority education advisers with information on strategies covering nursery education for three- and four-year-olds, with an emphasis on the four-year-olds. Again, neighbourhood discussion on what parents and children need from provision would be a good place from which to start to unpack assumptions about care and education, but there was little evidence that this type of discussion was taking place.

Another feature of the DfEE requirements, inherited from the voucher scheme, is that a qualified teacher should be involved in all funded provision for three- and four-year-olds and Standards Fund money has been available to support this. This was originally a contentious issue with non-maintained providers, and local authorities have had to be careful in their selection of the staff who will do this work and in the types of support schemes which have been devised. However, this is now firmly established within the initiative and the new guidance asks for details of how the involvement will operate to raise standards, particularly in the areas of activity planning, special needs and general assessment of children.

Partnership development

As has been mentioned earlier, partnership officers were frequently torn between the need to do groundwork with their own partnerships and the need to complete the heavy list of tasks in the guidance in a very short timescale. The pressure on partnership members was also great and coordinators reported some falling off in membership and, above all, a difficulty in recruiting independent chairs. Some experienced a lack of understanding on the part of elected members, and sometimes other officers, of the role and remit of the partnership and a reluctance – occasionally even outright hostility – over being asked to share responsibility with such a body. All of this points up yet again the importance of central government understanding such constraints and allowing for them, not by forcing players into a pre-arranged agenda of discussions, but by allowing the time and flexibility for ongoing debate and negotiation. Many coordinators hoped that the new development officers coming into post with childcare grants would free up their own time for partnership development. Again, this needs to be monitored.

Overall, the evidence from the work with partnerships and their officers this year reveals a mixed picture of enormous potential, twinned with disappointing progress, on exactly those issues which will affect the long-term viability of the work, that is:

- partnership development;
- corporate initiatives on the part of local authorities to support the work strategically;
- clear guidance from central government on the above local authority support;
- a systematic approach to community involvement in development;
- a systematic approach to auditing and consultation;
- the development of local recruitment, retention of staff and career strategies;
- the development of a national funding strategy which supports sustainability;
- community-based discussions on the nature and quality of services which meet people's needs. In Chapter 6, we make some suggestions about why such issues are vital and how they might be tackled.

Evidence from the audits

Our sources of information also showed that there were some very clear and consistent messages coming from the audits:

- Partnerships and coordinators were concerned about the response of central government to the audits.
- Very different situations were offered the same solutions, rural areas particularly feeling that the guidance had indirect urban bias, since all the solutions, targets and so on were ones which are only really feasible in urban areas.
- In the second round of letters to chief executives asking partnerships to increase their targets, a number responded that their targets were based on the audits and they were not prepared to increase them.
- Many of the audits found that there was no simple relationship between the provision of childcare and access to the labour market. Indeed, many of the audits identified a very low take-up of available childcare in the most disadvantaged areas.

- Similarly, many of the audits found that children often want to go home after school and actively do not want to have after-school care or clubs or anything else.
- Overwhelmingly, as expected, employers do not see what childcare has to do with them.

Conclusions

These sets of information seem to us to confirm what most of us already knew, that local authorities were not up to speed in understanding and carrying out their role as enablers and that none of the key stakeholders, with the exception of children, have a developed view of what the services should actually look like. More than this, however, they confirm the complexity of the issues which have been delegated to the partnerships and the need to acknowledge the **process** of partnership as the key dynamic, rather than the simple achievement of targets. What has been achieved is none-the-less impressive. Every authority now has a partnership, a plan and an audit. What remains to be seen is whether the partnerships themselves can rise above the dictates of performance management and revitalise their communities with creative local solutions to the fundamental issues in the relationship between work and the bringing up of children.

4 Achieving partnership

So what do we mean by the term 'partnership'? One eight-year-old, as a member of a school council, had consulted other eight-year-olds in the playground and identified the following priorities:

- wanting a lunchtime shop;
- a swimming pool (my friend said that, and I did say it back to the Council but the whole group just gave a chuckle and said 'I don't think so');
- stopping bullying and name calling;
- no locks on the boys' loos (Oliver asked me to bring that up);
- the need for some people to be potty trained again, because the boys weed on the walls and it made the toilets stinky for everyone;
- saying if you have been sick: someone had been and no one owned up;
- things in your lunchbox that you can eat quickly because you hardly get any time to have your lunch and, if you haven't finished you get told off by the dinner ladies;
- about all the boys pushing in the playground – 'Well it's the football children, so it's girls, too'.

ECU Audit/Partnership Project (January 1999)

This is a favourite example of a partnership approach to children. In this instance it is explicitly understood by both adults and children as an example of partnership, whereas in some of the following descriptions this may be, to some readers, less obvious. Our aim is to set out several different ways of understanding the components of partnership which will, or could, be at work at any one time in every early years development and childcare partnership. Our thinking is that many of the real strengths of the partnerships are still implicit and that, if they are explicitly acknowledged, there will be significant dividends.

The following sequence of photographs (Figures 4.1–4.4), taken at one of the internationally famous nurseries of Reggio Emilia in Italy, is another illustration of an excellent partnership – this time between an adult and a child. The pictures speak for themselves as Laura, aged

Figure 4.1 The 'Laura' series: Laura is 11-months-old, a pre-speaker, but is seen here engaged in a mutual exploration with her adult guide

The 'Laura' Series (pp. 56–59) is reproduced, with permission from the catalogue of the exhibition 'The Hundred Languages of Children'. © 1996 Municipality of Reggio Emilia – Infant-Toddler Centres and Preschools. Published by Reggio Children.

Figure 4.2 The 'Laura' series: And so the conversation continues ...

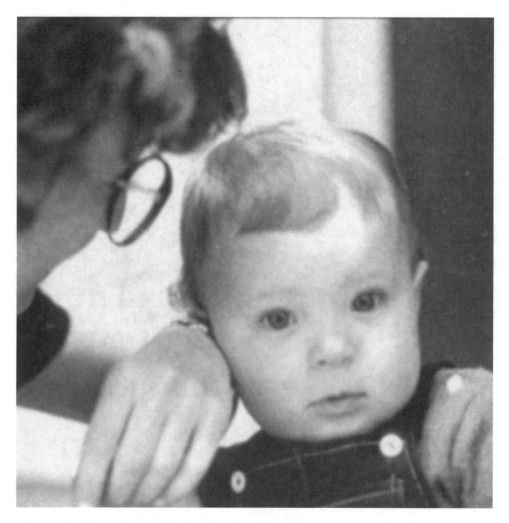

Figure 4.3 The 'Laura' series: And again ...

Figure 4.4 The 'Laura' series: Until Laura tests her latest theory

eleven months, works with the attentive pedagogue to structure her instinctive curiosity. Behind the everyday practice of Reggio, however, there is an intricate but nonetheless robust system of partnership, based on the belief that human relationships are the channel through which learning will take place, both for adults and for children.

> The concept of *'schooling as a system of relations'* which guides the work in Reggio Emilia produces much more than good feelings on the parts of those involved. Rather, this emphasis on relations represents a commitment to engagement in multiple levels of discourse among and between teachers and parents, schools and the larger community. The success with which parents, citizens and teachers in Reggio Emilia have negotiated their educational aims and processes based on shared understandings of their children provides compelling support for the premise that conceptions of quality and developmental appropriateness cannot be derived from formulaic interpretation of children's development, nor can personal or professional knowledge of children dominate the conversation. Rather, the determination of quality approaches to children's care and education requires a functional system of relations where divergent and minority voices count, with coordinated and collaborative efforts to improve everyone's *'image of the child'*. Ongoing documentation of children's learning, advocacy for children's rights, and the participation of all stakeholders – parents as well as other citizens of the community – will significantly contribute to this process and its outcomes.
>
> *R New (1998)*

Another way of describing this system of relations is, of course, as partnership and this is a recurrent theme across the world. In its simplest and most complex form, the African proverb *'It takes a whole village to educate a child'* is a clear statement of partnership. In the larger societies of the West, the forms of partnership may seem different but there are clear commonalities. In Hurd, Lerner and Barton, the features of effective programmes supporting families and children are explored:

> Teachers can make meaningful links with the larger community when they conceptualise their roles as multi-faceted resources for children, reflect on the complex needs of children and their families, recognise the contexts that people live in, and respect diversity.
>
> *T Hurd, R Lerner and C Barton (1999)*

They then go on to describe various models of partnership, including examples in which the university acts as an expert directly with the community group and they conclude:

> Early childhood teachers have long recognised the interdependent nature of teaching and supporting families. Partnerships with parents have been a primary focus of early childhood education since its inception. As we move toward broader community, business, agency and university partnerships, where resources are pooled in support of and in service to families, we can draw on lessons from individual teachers and from long-standing programs.

By meeting the needs of children through the provision of integrated services that represent partnerships of care and commitment we build on the skills and legacy of early childhood education.

T Hurd, R Lerner and C Barton (1999)

This same concept of partnership is the basis for the cross-cultural work in Canada of Pence and McCallum who describe their generative curriculum model as follows:

- a place where students are allowed to remain rooted in or near their communities and are not required to move far away for months or years at a time;
- a place where students can apply what they learn on a daily basis with their own people and in their own communities;
- a place where students can step off a career ladder to pursue professional employment and step back on to pursue degree work;
- a place where majority and First Nations information is valued;
- a place where a mainstream university and a First Nations Tribal Council work in cooperation, harmony and trust;
- a place where Elders play a key role in contributing to curriculum, to students' and to children's and communities' development;
- a place where students, Elders and teachers are all instructors and are all learners;
- a place where communities take the responsibility for defining and describing the care-giving practices and standards that they will follow;
- a place where strengths, rather than weaknesses, are considered the appropriate starting place for developing strong children, strong families and strong communities;
- a place that provides many new things to learn, not just for First Nations and universities, but more broadly for 'any community' and any post-secondary institution.

In short, what we have discovered thus far on our shared voyage is the outline of an alternative landscape – a land form influenced by a different set of principles than those we typically experience. It is a landscape that, in my opinion, offers great promise at a time when we need promising alternatives.

A Pence and M McCallum (1994)

This generative curriculum model was a partnership system designed to create the strongest possible alliance between staff and children in order to secure the cultural and economic identity of a First Nation Tribal Community in Canada.

Perhaps less elaborately, but certainly with considerable success, we see partnership at work in the Peers Early Education Partnership in Blackbird Lees in Oxford, where a curriculum for children from birth to age three is shared with parents and children within their own community and, at the same time, parents gain accreditation for their own learning. Figures 4.5 and 4.6 show a typical group and an event celebrating the award of accreditation certificates. The family learning groups of the

Figure 4.5 Early education partnership

Reproduced with permission from Peers Early Education Partnership, Blackbird Lees, 1999.

Figure 4.6 The PEEP accreditation ceremony

Reproduced with permission from Peers Early Education Partnership, Blackbird Lees, 1999.

Families and Schools Together Service in Sefton illustrate the same enthusiasm and mutuality. More recently, the community in Mereside in Blackpool engaged in the process of making a Sure Start Trailblazer application. Staff of the social services department were able to articulate a vision for the programme drawn from direct community involvement:

Choices

A place, within walking distance, where I could go and meet people, a place for a parent who hasn't got a child at school to meet people. It would have cheap meals and cups of tea and be open all day. There would be somewhere safe for the children to play with a nursery or crèche. I would be able to chat, or play with the children, or go shopping. Perhaps we could do aerobics or yoga. There would be an enclosed park, and things for children to do which wouldn't cost money. The whole family could go, and if you have three or four children they would all be catered for at the same time. We could go on trips, it would be like a family centre for everyone. Grannies could come and could adopt them. I don't have any family myself and my children miss that. It would be nice if there was a person there who I could talk to, tell my problems to, someone I could trust, who would know where I could go for advice without making an appointment. Or maybe people will call in, people who know about services. I wouldn't be nervous if there was someone there I trusted who could give me confidence, or could be an advocate.

J Rees, Mereside Sure Start Trailblazer application (1999)

From this vision they were able to articulate objectives for the programme, as follows.

In this community there are expressed wishes to:

- help ourselves and each other;
- make the vision of 'choices' and the related views of children about the services they need happen;
- have professionals who listen.

These aspirations have been used to lead the forming of the Sure Start Mereside Objectives:

- To maximise opportunities for parents to have friendly adult contact.
- To maximise opportunities for children to play together, by themselves and with their parents and other adults.
- To develop skills within the community which will maximise its capacity for decision-making about the content and quality of services, local governance of services, local provision of services and access to lifelong learning and employment
- To increase awareness and local pride through information exchange and collection.
- To have advocacy and personal counselling services available within the community.
- To build a programme of support for training from birth which maximises parental involvement and rewards it.

- To develop an approach to the delivery of services which promotes peer group support and outreach at all times.
- To make all local services as inclusive as possible for those who have special educational needs or who are disabled.

Mereside Sure Start Trailblazer application

Finally, attention should also be paid to the successful examples of large strategic partnerships. In Sheffield, for example, there is a city-wide partnership called Children Mean Business, which draws on European structural funds in the form of the European Regional Development Fund to develop and assist new childcare and other small businesses. The partnership brings together voluntary and private sector partners as well as the local authority within a system of relations.

Similarly, but on a larger scale, there is clear evidence of the effectiveness of partnerships in Northern Ireland. Figure 4.7 shows the structure in place there for a population of 1.5 million. Working within this, the Northern Ireland Pre-school Playgroups Association (NIPPA), one of the foremost early years organisations in the country, list the successes as:

- process of coming together;
- strategic focus at regional and area level;
- success in attracting significant European funding;
- systematic approach to assessment of need, auditing of services and targeting of resources;
- strategic approach to key issues which had fragmented the sector: training strategies, funding, capital infrastructure;
- synergy with other major initiatives: Children's Services Planning process, Childcare Strategy, New Opportunities Fund, Sure Start.

Coming even closer to home, we could characterise the Early Years Coordinators' Network as a partnership which, although it does not engage in a local practical project, has nevertheless forged over the years a way of working together and sharing experiences which it would be hard to replicate in any new and more deliberate structure. Old network 'hands' welcome in the many new coordinators who are joining the field at present and offer them a tried and trusted mechanism for obtaining practical support. They have constructed a way of talking together which is honest and challenging, while still being supportive. As one member of a regional grouping put it when they were about to embark on a discussion of a possible new and very radical strategy: 'We need to have this debate when we know we are among friends/ partnerships'.

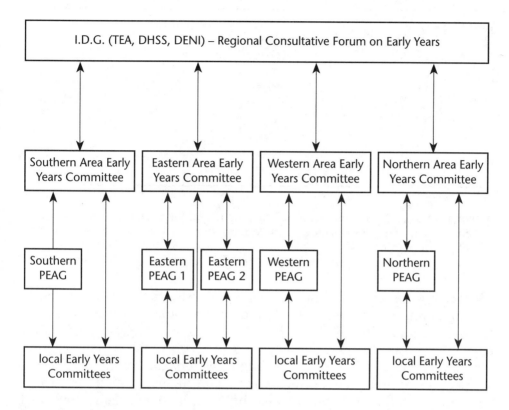

Figure 4.7 Partnership across Northern Ireland

Reproduced with the permission of Siobhan Fitzpatrick (Chief Executive of Northern Ireland Pre-school Playgroups Association).

Our examples of success, therefore, move from child to child partnerships through adult/child partnerships with communities, whole cities and whole regions. What they have in common is mutuality and respect, the sharing of valued resources and aspiration and a willingness to be adventurous: to boldly go where no man, woman or child has gone before!

5 The third way?

'We need to find ways for "welfare" to support valued activities such as caring, volunteering and education alongside paid work, if we are to foster social as well as human capital.'

Carey Oppenheim, The Guardian *(29 September 1999)*

The above was one of three fundamental recommendations made by Oppenheim in suggesting how New Labour should continue to reshape the welfare state. Building on what she saw as 'an ambitious and radical agenda which sees work as a route out of poverty; a role for redistribution via tax credits and a stronger emphasis on the responsibilities of claimants through tougher sanctions and firmer action on fraud'. Oppenheim's other proposals were that people should leave jobs with more skills than they started with and that the nature of the contributory principle should be changed, for example, by applying the model of the individual learning accounts to other needs such as parental leave. This is a clear example of the opening up of debate about the place of caring including the bringing up of children in relation to work and the welfare relationships which support those who cannot or should not have to work.

For those of us who are involved in the formation of the Early Years Development and Childcare Partnerships and who care about the future of our children, this kind of public debate is urgently needed if policy is to move forward in ways which reflect real lives rather than the dominant paradigm. This is especially true at local level where so much of the business of living is tied up with the delivery of critically needed services. As we know, however, the services often bypass the vitality of children; many of whom survive despite their environment rather than because of the support it gives. However, a large number of children are not managing. Suicide, drug addiction, homelessness and poverty affect at least a third of all our children, the clearest possible sign that things are not just not 'joined-up' but seriously, badly wrong. Work in itself will not get children out of this. What is needed, as Oppenheim says, is a whole new set of acknowledged and valued interdependencies.

What our work tells us is that this debate has come to the boil in the new partnerships. Our fragmented and much scorned patchwork of services has within it a potent mixture of passion and enlightened self-interest. Our history is awash with exemplars of success and over the past 30 years there have been dramatic advances in learning about how to deliver services that help rather than hinder or hurt. What is needed now is a sustained and serious conversation at a local level with ourselves and our children, to assess what we know and what we don't know. Much of what we have found in the partnerships is naked self-interest and territoriality, the continuance of the mechanisms of inequality. There is, however, so much more which is often emotional sometimes evangelical but also purposeful and informed which desperately needs to be trusted and engaged with.

So how should we proceed? We have come to think that there are several persistent messages in the work we have described so far which offer a way forward.

The significance of process

Our experience to date is that the tasks which are technically the responsibility of partnerships are taxing and complex. They require not only a significant level of time, energy and commitment, but also an ability to reflect, discuss and plan together honestly as a group. In many cases, the groundwork required to build such functional and dynamic groups has not been undertaken in the pressured timetable of the Labour Government's first two years. Some partnerships are experiencing difficulties in recruiting or keeping voluntary and private sector members, in finding independent chairs or in achieving good attendance. Many others rely overwhelmingly on local authority officers, not just for servicing and procedural advice but also for the development of service plans and all too often we find that any sense of wholeness is lost in the rush to get words on paper.

We would argue that partnership development should be given the highest priority, have mandatory systems of self-assessment and as a minimum have these interlinked aims and objectives:

- long-term support to enable a diverse range of partners to work together successfully;
- acknowledging and maintaining the partnership as a dynamic process which can attract and harness active participation rather than reproduce the committee systems of existing bureaucracies;
- clear definition of tasks and goals and clear programmes for delivering on them and monitoring progress derived from shared understanding and negotiation;

- clear mechanisms for meaningful community involvement, taking account of geographic communities, communities of interest and communities of identity;
- clear ways of envisioning hopes and dreams;
- ways of making things happen and achieving change.

Convergent agendas

The EYDC Partnerships interact with a whole range of agendas:

- reduction in crime and disorder;
- poverty and social exclusion;
- economic regeneration, particularly the issue of uneven development within individual regions and towns;
- the need to develop a skilled labour force;
- the raising of educational standards for schoolchildren;
- issues of equality between minority ethnic and social groups;
- the improvement of childcare for working parents, particularly issues of affordability, availability and the integration of care and education;
- the improvement of preventative childcare services for families under stress.

They represent without doubt a project of enormous social significance and yet central government acknowledges these connections only as an afterthought.

The articulated task for the partnerships is to set up more provision, but they are in fact a focal point for all the above issues and offer a prime forum for discussion and negotiation of some of the most pressing social projects, most particularly those concerning the resolution of work/family dilemmas. As such our partnerships equate with the partnerships in Reggio or in the Meadow Lake Tribal Community. We would therefore argue that the centrality of the partnerships as a means of engaging locally appropriate practice across all of the service disciplines should be immediately acknowledged and they should be owned and serviced by all government departments rather than just by the DfEE.

The bringing up of children

The nature of the bringing up of children in the modern world is challengingly complex or 'wicked' to use the jargon of social policy. Furthermore, children are the most powerless members of our society and can all too often be discounted by us, the adults, at the same time as we fear their behaviour and doubt our ability to control it. The recent government emphasis on parenting and on supporting parents to do a better job has assumed that parents need to be 'educated' into parenthood and that their improved performance will have a beneficial effect on a range of social problems including educational standards, crime and disorder, poor health, and benefit dependence. As the Mereside parents quoted in Chapter 4 show us, there is an articulated need for more support and resources for parents, but this is a need which must be negotiated at local level in a way which will provide local solutions and local assessments of what is or is not working. Here again, the partnerships have a unique role and should be seen as a central mechanism for the delivery of support to parents. Consultation should not be limited to identifying simplistic measures of demand for childcare but rather be a persistent and locally important part of the bringing up of children.

Renewing democracy

Thirdly, there is the question of democracy and the involvement of people in community and civic life. Increasingly over the last decade the electorate has avoided the ballot box, so that now some local and European elections have ludicrously low rates of turnout. As there has been an increasing polarisation between the work-rich (with few hours to spare outside the workplace) and the work-poor (with few resources), so traditional community activities such as volunteering, evening classes and social clubs have diminished. New forums need to be found to engage people once again in civic life and in the community rather than the individual or the family. Central government has recognised this with its 'modernisation' agenda for local government, a two-pronged attack on traditional local authority practice designed to make governance more attractive and accessible to ordinary people while also breaking the hegemony of traditional 'Old Labour' behaviour and beliefs.

Again, partnership working is central to this agenda, offering a new way of influencing and implementing policy and providing an avenue for civic involvement. Dahlberg, Moss and Pence's description of how this type of function could be undertaken by early childhood institutions could relate just as well to an EYDC Partnership:

> [institutions as forums] can serve multiple purposes: as a means of *inclusion* for children and adults, in civil society; creating opportunities for *the exercise of democracy and freedom*, through learning, dialogue and critical thinking; offering wide-ranging and flexible forms of *social support* for parents, both in and out of the labour market; and providing a mechanism of *redistribution* of resources towards children as a social group.
>
> *G Dahlberg, P Moss and A Pence (1999) pp. 80–1*

The ECU Audit/Partnership Project, which provided some of the information on which this publication is based, is described in Appendix 1. One of the mechanisms developed within that project was the idea of the 'community partnership' being a vehicle for implementing the work of the EYDC Partnerships. Figure 5.1 depicts the possible membership of such a community partnership at very local level and the ways in which it can address the agendas and funding streams of central government. Such local partnerships can then link directly into the work of the authority-wide partnership providing both a focus and conduit for development of childcare places as well as a more consistent and representative consultation mechanism. EYDC Partnerships may also wish to ensure that they have additional representation from specific community groups (such as minority ethnic communities) or interest groups if it is felt that their needs would not be adequately represented by the community partnerships.

Community partnerships do offer a more effective mechanism for consulting with parents, an issue which has taxed many partnerships.

Potential resources
Early Years and Childcare Development Funds
Further Education Funding Council
European Structural Funds
Local Investment Fund
Regeneration Funds
Public/Private Finance

Figure 5.1 An area/community partnership network of services

Reproduced with the permission of the National Children's Bureau from *Planning Partnership and Equality for Young Children* (1998).

One or two people who just happen to be parents (often parent governors have been suggested) cannot be fully representative of parental interests, as they can only speak as individuals. Alternatively, community partnerships can bring together parents as consumers of local services in an area small enough to facilitate meaningful consultation between parents and stakeholders through 'word of mouth' networks. These indeed give some legitimate basis and real context for their views. Individuals from the constituent community partnerships and members of the authority-wide partnerships can then be brought together in a 'parent college'. This college can be considered a consultation mechanism, but also as a tool for channelling the views of several parents to the EYDC Partnerships (a model depicted in Figure 5.2 outlining a possible partnership structure).

Similarly, Figure 5.3 shows the structure of Bristol's partnership. Local networks feed in, as do the subject-based subgroups. This structure links to the audit of existing local networks, part of Bristol's childcare audit

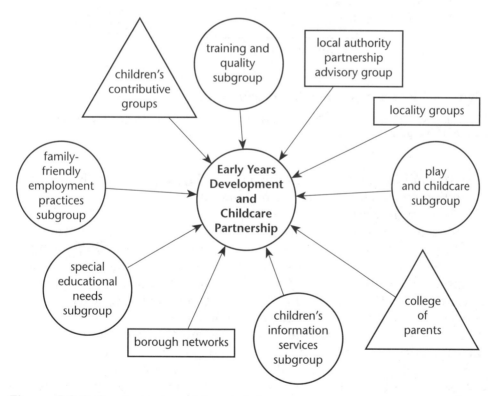

Figure 5.2 Sefton's partnership model

Reproduced with permission from Sefton's Early Years and Development and Childcare Partnership Plan working papers 1999–2000.

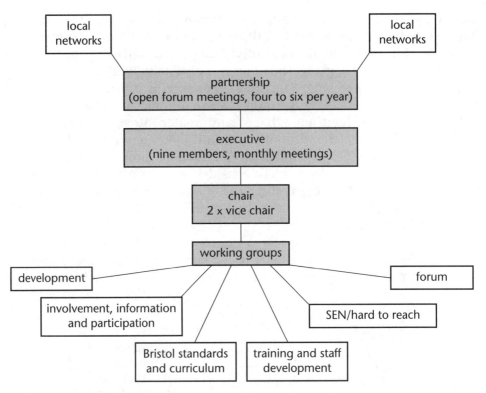

Figure 5.3 Bristol's partnership organisation

Reproduced with permission from Bristol's Early Years and Development and Childcare Partnership Plan working papers 1999–2000.

(see Appendix 1), and provided the partnership with an effective shortcut to finding out about local developments and to formulating an ongoing consultation network.

The community partnership, deployed as a strategic mechanism, encourages us to believe that the tension between work and the bringing up of children can be resolved within a local context without compromising efficiency targets. The more in-depth and systematic consultation, which the model supports, strengthens capacity building and thereby routes to economic sustainability.

The first essential action step, therefore, must be to explore the idea of **partnership.** It must be examined, understood and then **adopted** as the way to do things by all of the stakeholders. This involves a great deal more than words on paper. If we are to be certain of achieving partnership, we need to negotiate our terms of reference first and examine the values which we bring to the project. This is more than agreeing where and at what times meetings are to be held (although this is always a place to start). It means, as our colleagues in Sutton have said, 'debating what partnership means' and then designing the indicators to measure performance (London Borough of Sutton, 1999). All of this is within the power of the new partnerships if they are given the time to do it and the significance of this activity is recognised and enabled by government.

It is equally essential to have recognition at central government level of the complexity and potential of the agenda facing the partnerships. Despite the startling convergence of issues around the uniting theme of early childhood care and education, policy from central government is still compartmentalised and, it often seems, competitive. Policy on children and families seems all too often to appear as an adjunct to the other more 'serious' strategies. A government department which could look at the totality of bringing up children by implementing joined-up thinking would address this deficient policy making.

There needs to be an explicit recognition of the tasks which need to be undertaken prior to, or alongside, the development of childcare places. These include: partnership development and strategic development of quality standards, consultation forums and lifelong learning. This would enable partnerships to meet targets in a sustainable manner and in ways more likely to ensure community stability. This would not be a 'soft option'. Debate and development of this nature, if it is to be productive, requires tightly managed performance criteria, an ability to assess progress and clear channels for informing (and being informed by) practice.

The positive result of this process will be a building of capacity at community level which will eventually benefit everyone. A form of local provision can then be developed which is sharply responsive to need and tailored to the funding streams supporting the agendas of government, such as New Deal, Supporting the Family, Raising Standards and so on in mutually beneficial ways. This means bringing the lessons of the Educational Priority Areas, the Community Development Projects and the Regeneration Partnerships forward into today's society and combining them with the skill and expertise which has been developed over the years by our patchwork of providers.

The community partnership model has, at its heart, the power of participation, communication and debate. DfEE Guidance (1999) tells us that two of the aims of the partnerships should be to: 'be directed by the diverse needs and aspirations of children locally, and of their parents, and pay attention to the support of families' and 'generate genuine partnership and debate between all providers and others, and seek agreement how needs can best be met'. It is now time to unravel and explore what this means in words and deeds. It would be self-defeating to feel that such rhetoric marks the so called 'political ceiling' beyond which we are not invited to explore.

Just as Robert Owen gave us a wonderful starting point, so the Meadow Lake Tribal Council gives us a bridge to the future. Robert Owen was not only a visionary he was also the boss, head of the organisation. Children at New Lanark had music lessons in the nursery because he believed it was good for them. The fact that he was right was just good luck for the families who worked for him and, as we all know, there are many instances where bosses or leaders have got it, or are getting it, wrong. But the Meadow Lake Tribal Council have not relied on the vision and resources of one individual. They have pushed back the frontiers of democracy by insisting on an approach to the teaching of their children based on serious, systematic partnership, power sharing and debate.

Essentially, the story of the Meadow Lake Tribal Council is that their initial emphasis on economic development had not always been successful, in part because of the lack of skilled and motivated First Nations people to do the work.

> We realised that if we wanted to develop economically we first had to develop our human resources. Because development must come from the inside, not the outside.
>
> *Vern Bachiu, Programs and Policy Director with the*
> *Meadow Lake Tribal Council*

A social worker was then employed to do what we might describe as capacity building but which she described as 'they asked us to dream the best possible child care program we could imagine. And so we did'. These beginnings led to a partnership with the University of Victoria which resulted in a process, driven by the MLTC and involving Elders from the communities, for devising a new format of curriculum (described as a generative model) to guide the training of local people in childcare. The process involved extensive direct conversations between the local people and academics on an ongoing basis. What followed was a remarkable rediscovery of identity and self-worth for everyone who took part.

This need not only be the stuff of dreams.

> 'It isn't just a dream that we can reinforce people believing that they sink or swim together, that they themselves can flourish better if they are doing it in tandem, mutuality.'
>
> *David Blunkett, Secretary of State for Education and Employment,*
> *Sure Start Trailblazer Conference (Sure Start, 1999).*

There is already much in our provision which has begun like this (see Chapter 4). There is also new money, and young children have a higher profile than ever before. The history of the reconciliation of work and the bringing up of children is not good in the UK and, with more than a third of all children being brought up in conditions of social exclusion and poverty, this is something which we cannot continue to get wrong. Like the Meadow Lake communities, our future is at stake. At the same time, well intentioned as we all may be, we are up to our necks in paper plans. We are being driven by targets for expansion which do not reflect the locally collected information about demand. In short, we could be about to throw the baby out with the bath water. However, so much more is possible if we are serious about sustained economic renewal and recognise that it is inextricably linked with the social project of childcare and education – if, to repeat Robert Owen, we truly wish to 'unite a great variety of parts to produce one grand result'.

First Nations of the Meadow Lake Tribal Council believe that a childcare program developed, administered and operated by their own people is a vital component to their vision of sustainable growth and development. It impacts every sector of their long-term plans as they prepare to enter the twenty-first century. It will be children who inherit the struggle to retain and enhance the people's culture, language, and history; who continue the quest for economic progress for a better quality of life; and who move forward with a strengthened resolve to plan their own destiny.

Children are our Future, Meadow Lake Tribal Council and University of Victoria School of Child and Youth Care, Curriculum Development Project

Appendix 1. Description of the Early Childhood Unit's Childcare Audit Partnership Project 1998–99

Introduction

Following the issuing of the draft guidance in Summer 1998, the Early Childhood Unit at the National Children's Bureau, along with many other early years organisations and consultants, was approached by a large number of EYDC partnerships to tender for the job of producing all or part of their childcare audit. The approach usually came from the local authority officer convening the partnership and varied considerably according to the state of development of the information systems within the local authorities. With money to spend on the audits, it was possible for partnerships to contract out all the audit work or to assess their own capabilities and supplement these with varying degrees of support or with specific tasks, for example, the consultation exercises. However, none of the tenders sent to us seemed to address the central issue of how the partnership would relate to the audit in the development of the plan's priorities nor how the local authority would relate to the new centrality of the partnership. The majority assumed the audit to be a discrete one-off task, which could be farmed out to an external person with little consideration of how it articulated with the rest of the process. In some cases, even individual bits of the audit, particularly consultation exercises, were treated in this way.

In the event, we decided to take a proactive stance and to invite local authorities/ partnerships to join a development partnership, if they were interested in working with our approach. This also allowed us to integrate the project very clearly into the prospectus of work which the Unit is currently pursuing. This includes the practice development and dissemination work connected with the Early Years Coordinators' Network, a forum serviced by the Unit which brings local authorities into regular contact with each other and with us at national and regional meetings and at seminars and conferences. Linkages can therefore be developed around geographical or subject areas and local authorities – and now partnerships – can learn informally from each other or can develop more formal, funded projects for taking work forward. Representatives of this network now also attend the national meetings of the Early Childhood Education Forum (ECEF) and so can, additionally, form linkages with voluntary and private sector national organisations around such projects. It was this type of cross-partnership work which we were anxious to develop in response to the audit requirement, in order to ensure that a group of local authorities/partnerships could pool their experience and ideas for mutual benefit. This would mean that the audit could be located within the other work of partnership and plan development, and that the Unit could then disseminate the results more widely for the benefit of others, including the DfEE.

Project description

The project had to encompass the need of local authorities to do the following in a very short space of time:
- complete all the tasks connected with the audit and plan;
- develop new partnerships with the capacity to grow;
- put in place ongoing mechanisms for auditing, consulting and planning.

Our approach, therefore, incorporated an anticipated capacity for ongoing community level planning and we approached the audits with the following aims:
- to identify and link existing data sets;
- to combine this quantitative information with new and existing sources of qualitative information, including consultation and community-led assessments of need;
- to establish audits as vehicles through which the aggregated information could inform and support change at all levels from the bottom to the top.

The Early Childhood Unit assembled a consortium with complementary skills, which could work with a group of partnerships and their respective local authorities to prepare meaningful audits within the prescribed timescales. It could also begin to establish or strengthen the planning processes and technical infrastructure necessary to sustain continuous integrated development, including consultation and public information systems.

The core partners group comprised the following organisations and representatives:
- Department of Applied Social Studies and Social Research, University of Oxford (Teresa Smith)
- National Childminding Association (Gill Haynes)
- Working for Childcare (Vanessa Schepers)

Between them, the partners had expertise in data collection and analysis, electronic mapping and other electronically-assisted systems for the analysis and dissemination of information; the development and integration of planning structures, particularly in the early years field; consultation work with employers, parents and children; and the development of public information services. They also held existing data sets on childminding, employer-supported childcare, early years training and qualifications and good practice in local authority early years services, all of which we planned to utilise as part of this project.

An outline of our approach to the audit work was then sent to all those partnerships which had expressed an interest in working with us. It included the following elements:
- The Early Childhood Unit will engage with the group of local authorities and partnerships within specific contractual arrangements to meet the needs of each authority. These could include any of the following, as required:
  - identification and integration of existing sources of quantitative and qualitative data;
  - configuration of an appropriate electronically-assisted system for the routine analysis and dissemination of the information;
  - identification and analysis of fitness for purpose of existing planning structures (via structured interviews with key personnel);
  - design of locality-based consultation processes which interact with the above systems of data collection and planning;
  - integration of the audit and consultation information into childcare and early years plans;

- development of ongoing action plans to implement the strategic planning arising from the above exercise over a longer timescale and over a wider range of activities.
- Each authority was asked to bring together a project team to work with representatives of the core partners to undertake the audit and action planning work within their respective authorities and partnerships. Practice development and exchange was to occur within developmental meetings held over the period of the partnership programme.

Aims

To maximise the impact of the childcare audit for each of the participating authorities and partnerships and to contribute to the national development of good practice.

Outputs

Working audit and action plan for each of the participating authorities and a national evaluation report.

Outcomes

An enhanced holistic base for the development of children's services.

In the event, six local authorities responded positively to the proposal and they were a varied group representing urban and rural, large and small, unitary (both new and old) and two-tier authorities. However, in terms of the way in which they organised children's services, these authorities were more homogeneous. Some had done preparatory work towards reorganising local authority structures in order to deliver integrated services and/or management, but none had actually done it. All had drafted in new or additional staff or had extended the contracts of short-term posts in order to cover this work. Our discussions within the Coordinators' Network led us to believe that this was not unrepresentative of local authority teams.

They initially identified staff who would attend the development group meetings and, in subsequent discussions with Unit staff, identified full project teams to work on the audit and planning tasks. All were local authority officers rather than other partnership members. Early Childhood Unit staff took responsibility for specific areas of work and the core partners (ECU, Oxford, NCMA and WfC) attended planning meetings of their own as well as all the development group meetings. Outside these, the main work took place in individual authorities/partnerships as the audits and plans took shape. One new unitary authority later decided that the project was not meeting its needs and withdrew. The remaining five authorities/partnerships continued with the project and later built additional work onto the original specification, most usually in connection with parents and children's consultation processes and partnership development.

The work in practice

The mentoring approach

The main feature of the project was that of mentoring and this took place in the following activities.

Development group meetings

This indicates meetings of the project as a whole, involving the consortium partners and representatives from each participating authority/partnership. They were designed as forums for sharing information and practice, reflection and review, problem-solving and feedback on national, local and project developments.

Local authority project initiation and project development meetings

Within each local authority project team, these meetings were to set the parameters of the audit tasks, identify the roles and responsibilities of team members, allocate tasks and review and monitor the progress of the work.

Fact finding

Initial survey of existing information and processes for planning, data collection and analysis, including fitness for purpose of existing electronic data systems. Identification of information required from consortium members such as National Childminding Association and Working for Childcare.

Information synthesis

Advice and support on demographics, geographical information systems (GIS) and other socio-spatial planning tools, consultation processes and planning structures. Inclusion of specific consortium sources of information such as NCMA database, employer information from Working for Childcare and training and qualification information from the HERA 2 database. The team was to use the services of IT consultants on this work, if necessary and appropriate.

The database approach

The audit is to be an ongoing process involving annual updates. In addition, partnerships need very clear and organised information from the audit on which to base their judgements about expansion. For both these reasons, it seemed clear to us that the information, once collected, should be stored on one interactive database which could be continually interrogated for different requirements and from which the information could be presented in different ways.

Even though this makes the audit much easier in the long run, it is a big task to undertake in a tight timescale and there was little innovation in this respect in the childcare audits which we have seen. This is not unexpected: there is always a tension between getting a task done and establishing systems that will manage this and similar tasks in the future. That tension is sharper when deadlines are tight and maybe the bodies charged with the task – the childcare partnerships – are themselves new and not yet bedded down.

The local authorities in this project appreciated the need for such a system and, although not all were able to put it in place before the plans, there are one or two very good examples from this group. Figure A.1 shows a summary from Sefton's audit, while Tables A1.1 and A1.2 show a page of information on which such a summary draws. Each ward profile drew on approximately 25 data sets, bringing them all together electronically in this way, so that they could be readily interrogated for ward-level data. This could also be done for any other unit of analysis which had been chosen, such as postcodes.

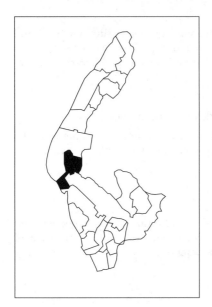
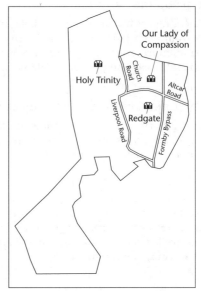

Figure A1.1 Area profile of Ravenmeols ward

Ravenmeols is the southern-most ward of Formby. It has a population of 11,700 residents.
  Ravenmeols has:
- a ranking of 21 out of 23 wards in terms of deprivation (Townsend Deprivation Score);
- a low standard rate of 15 for those living in terraced housing;
- a ward ranking of 22 out of 23 wards for those unemployed and for lone parent claimants;
- a low population of children 0–14 with a ranking of 20 out of 23 wards.

Table A1.1 Number of children with a statement of special educational needs in Ravenmeols ward

Area	Total no. children aged 0–14	Total no. under-14s with a statement of SEN	Rate (%)	SR
Ravenmeols total	1531	29	2.6	84
Borough total	49798	1104	100	100

Source: Educational Management System: Special Education Needs Module Sefton MBC (November 1998)

Table A1.2 Number of children allocated to a social worker in Ravenmeols ward

Area	Total no. children aged 0–14	Total no. under-14s with a statement of SEN	Rate (%)	SR
Ravenmeols total	1531	14	1.6	52
Borough total	49798	868	100	100

Source: Client Record System (CRISSP) Social Services, Department Sefton MBC (December 1998)

The potential advantages of a well-designed database system include:
- The option of continuous updating throughout the year, providing key planning information for the partnership and any local groups and enabling the following year's audit to be completed more easily.
- Having just one set of data, for instance the live births figures, stored in one place with all the tables that draw on that information, automatically updating when the data is changed.
- Being able to generate labels or mail-merged letters to any of the organisations listed in the audit. One obvious application would be to produce letters automatically two or three times a year to all the providers listed, setting out the information currently stored and asking for corrections and updates.
- Automatic recalculation of totals, percentages, standard ratios, and so on when data is changed or corrected. For example, if a playgroup has been booked against the wrong area and this information is corrected, a database system will correct not only the listing of this facility, but also the total number of places in both areas and any tables or charts comparing the numbers of places with the numbers of children.
- User-friendly screens for adding or changing information that can check the data as it is entered, making sure that a postcode is valid or that the area telephone code is correct.
- The option of changing the small areas in the light of developing experience. If the data stored is referenced to postcodes, census enumeration districts or polling districts, one table can record the names of the small areas used by the partnership and the postcodes or districts that make up each area. Changing this one table will relink to the other data and produce reports based on the new areas.
- The option of developing a range of reports, all drawing on the same data but, for instance, offering much more detail to local planning groups than might be appropriate for the annual report to the DfEE. A partnership could also generate specific information about need and provision in particular areas for private or voluntary sector partners considering new or expanded provision. Partnerships may also in this way use the same database to support applications to other funding regimes.

The initial project plan was written in September 1998, but had to be revised fairly soon after, as it became clear that existing information systems were not going to be able to cope with the deadlines demanded in the guidance. Also, in each of the local authorities, the individual pieces of work came in for constant rescheduling, as the project teams came up against limitations of time and data. This placed very real constraints on the way in which the audit could be used; it could not, as the guidance had envisaged, be completed, considered and used by whole partnerships in the development of plan targets and priorities.

Uniting features of the work

Within the overall framework and vision of the project, the work unfolded differently in different authorities but the uniting features (all of which were present in the DfEE guidance) were as follows:

Content of the audit
- collection of material on a database to enable updating and to offer a variety of ways of mapping the resulting information (see above);
- the role and method of children's and parents' consultation.

Process of the audit

- a mentoring approach to the work (see above);
- linkage of the audit with plan and partnership development processes.

Service development

- a locality development approach to planning and delivering services;
- the development of the local authority vision;
- the development of action plans to take the work forward beyond this period and to integrate it with other initiatives in the field of family support, lifelong learning and regeneration.

Appendix 2. Children's participation in the Early Childhood Unit's Childcare Audit Partnership Project 1998–99

Introduction

Consultation with children and young people about their preferences was a constituent part of the audit. This was a very welcome expectation in the planning guidance issued by the DfEE, but discussion in the Early Years Coordinators' Network had indicated a paucity of examples of effective consultation across the country and it was recognised that there were few places in which effective participation could be secured before the writing of this plan. A starting point for the project's core partners was that this participatory work with children should be central to the audit, the plan and the development of services in general within each partnership. Our aim was to support the partnerships involved, to consider the existing role of children in service planning in their area, to think about how this could be built upon and to develop new processes to improve the way in which children were consulted and informed. The intention was, and is, that consultation with all stakeholders should be integral to the planning process, reflecting both the method and the geographical unit in which services are planned and delivered, rather than add-on exercises covering wide geographical areas and having to be repeated every time a plan needs to be produced.

Children's participation within the guidance

The DfEE guidance (1999) indicated that plans should include:
- a description of steps taken to obtain the views of children and young people and the extent to which these are reflected in the overall plan (para. 61);
- particular attention to the views of older children, children with disabilities and children of minority ethnic origin (para. 62);
- how feedback is given to children and young people about the findings of the consultations and how their views have been incorporated into the local childcare plan (para. 63).

Guidance also has some useful points on the process of children's participation:
- Effective consultation with children is a long-term process. If they are to express their views effectively, children need to develop their:
  - knowledge of the issues that affect them;
  - own understanding of their right to be heard;
  - experience of sharing their views; and
  - confidence in expressing themselves.

- Children may only be able to contribute significantly to future plans and a more limited consultation may be the most realistic objective this time round (para. 64).
- It is important to recognise that the perspectives of children and adults will be different, but also that children's and adults' interests do not necessarily conflict (para. 65).
- It is better to ask children *about* services than to ask them to choose *between* services.
- Do not assume that children and young people are not also concerned about cost, availability, educational and learning opportunities (para. 67).
- This time round (that is, 1999/2000) the plan builds on existing mechanisms; next time, there will be considerable scope for creativity and innovation.
- There is a variety of methods such as children's, and young people's consultation forums; surveys; focus groups and interviews; creative and expressive activities.

The guidance also makes reference to the underpinning role of the UN Convention (para. 63).

Implementation of the guidance has inevitably been variable. Our impression, from our direct contacts with local authorities and partnerships, and from discussions with the regional network of local authority coordinators, is that firstly there has been too much pressure to complete the quantitative and statistical data for the audit to give much attention to children's views. Secondly, the very people who should be planning the long-term, integrated mechanisms for local consultation are those who have had the least time to do it, that is, the officers who have been setting up the partnerships and writing the plans.

But there is little doubt about the support and enthusiasm that exists for this part of the guidance. People responsible for compiling the plans have invariably been energised by discussions of this aspect of the work. This indicates that it is a relief to work on a part of the plan which is not heavily statistical and that it refocuses onto children's interests in a way which has been lacking in the implementation of some of the new policies and strategies, particularly the childcare strategy.

What's happening already?

One of the ways we have been assisting partnerships to address children's participation is to begin to identify in each area some of the activities already happening. We were surprised at the extent of children's participation that we found, although less surprised that much of it seemed to be happening in isolation. In each of the five local authority areas which were part of the project, there was at least some activity to take account of children's views. At the most basic level, these activities included:

- service providers taking account of children's preferences in the day-to-day planning of activities;
- inspectors specifically talking to children as part of the inspection process or trying to observe what children might be communicating non-verbally about their experience within a service;
- staff opportunely noting comments made by children about their own service or another, for example, children in nursery talking about their experience of the after-school club and vice versa.

At the other end of the spectrum, there appeared to be quite sophisticated activity to gather children's views in a way that was more conscious of age range and children's abilities. Particularly noteworthy seemed to be the work done through school councils and the possibilities of child-to-child research. In one authority, child members of a school council were invited to comment on some questions that a researcher had prepared about after-school activities. These questions were then changed or modified in the light of the children's comments and the children themselves used them to ask the views of other children.

In addition to the use of existing activities, these local authorities also mounted some large-scale consultation exercises specifically for the audit. In one, for instance, a private market research company was commissioned to ask children's views on a range of services and, although this particular exercise encountered some problems, there were some useful findings which the partnership intends to use in its service planning and its future consultations (see below):

Findings

From such exercises, a wide range of issues and examples emerged, for instance:

- views about wanting a wider range of after-school options than just *the* after-school club, for example, the possibility of spending more time in each others' homes;
- a strong feeling amongst children of all ages using after-school provision that they did not want to mix with children of a different age group;
- children's experiences of the statementing process and the extent of their under-standing about concepts, the roles of the various professionals they had to encounter, and their opportunities to contribute their own preferences to the process;
- three- and four-year-olds voting on play themes in nursery.

What seems so unique about these initiatives is that the conversations that ensue and the concerns and priorities that arise have a freshness and vitality that is both surprising and expected at the same time. Surprising, perhaps, because we are so unaccustomed to consulting children in a serious way. Expected because of the shock of recognition in what children tell us and what they prioritise. This point is well illustrated by the quotation given at the start of Chapter 4.

But if the vitality and freshness of these children's voices were common in each area, what also seemed to be common was the difficulty in achieving a systematic policy, strategy or methodology across early years services. Unless activities to give children a voice are linked together and then linked clearly into a planning process, children's voices are unlikely to impact on plans or make any significant difference.

In this respect, it is encouraging that there is a large and growing number of references on ethical processes for hearing children's voices in planning and research. Priscilla Alderson, in an overview commissioned by Barnardo's, lists ten critical topics to consider in consulting children as part of service evaluations as well as more formal research. We have reproduced them here because they seemed to us to provide a rigorous and helpful protocol for interrogating proposed activities to consult children.

The ten critical topics are:

- The purpose of the research: for example, whose interests is it designed to serve?
- Assessing the risks/benefits of children either participating or not participating.
- Privacy and confidentiality.
- Which children have been selected to participate and why? Who has been excluded?
- Remuneration: should children be paid?
- Do children have a voice in the methods used?
- Is information about aims and service options good enough?
- How is consent sought from children and from parents and what if they disagree?

- Will children get to know the outcomes of their participation?
- What are the underlying assumptions about children in the research, for example, about the quality, reliability and status of their views?

P Alderson (1995)

These are all challenging questions and alongside much of the other material that has been written on process, they give us a powerful framework in which to develop a more consistent strategy for incorporating children's views into research. But, as existing piecemeal approaches are made more systematic, some anxieties about giving children an effective voice emerge, too. We encountered two main kinds of anxiety.

In one local authority, some elected members were reported to have been very concerned that talking to children about the services they used was cutting across the role of parents. They worried that it is parents who have a responsibility to reconcile what children want with what they, as parents, believe they should receive or what they feel is manageable, given all the family circumstances. For instance, what if a child does not want to be in an after-school-club, but parents feel it is vital in order for them to hold down a job?

The second related anxiety is that it may not always be easy or manageable for parents to 'hear' that children's experience in services is not entirely positive, especially if they feel powerless to change the service or guilty that they let their child use it in the first place. The Unit's study of legal cases brought under the Children Act and evidence from many registration and inspection officers show that, in appeals to cancel registration of providers considered below standard, it is often parents who campaign on behalf of the provider (Elfer and Beasley, 1997).

We do not describe these anxieties in any way to make a case against children's participation. However, it is clearly vital to think about the anxieties which children's participation provokes, in order to prepare effective responses which allow for the enfranchisement of both children and parents and to think through the location and type of the forums in which such discussions can be carried out.

These anxieties serve a wider purpose, too. Anne Smith, working on children's participation in New Zealand, reminds us of the need to be conscious of how we see children and childhood:

- Are children just small adults, with less of everything; less knowledge, less experience and less wisdom, or is their perspective on the organisation of services no less valid than adults', but genuinely different and therefore valid in its own right?
- Are children more or less empty vessels to be filled up with the kinds of experiences and services we think it is appropriate to offer them, perhaps marginally fine-tuned by their own views and preferences?
- Are children only appendages in services that are really intended to fulfil adults' needs or objectives?

A B Smith (1995)

Conclusions

Anne Smith asks whether children's participation will just become another example of a conversation amongst 'us' about 'them'? This wider view suggests many exciting challenges for innovation by partnerships in having conversations 'directly' with children. For example, how children's views, not just adults' interpretations of children's views but gathered through research planned and conducted by children, might be communicated directly to partnership members; and how the plan can be demonstrably different because of the inclusion of the direct views of children.

One model of consultation which would arise from the developmental process inherent in our project would be for children's or schools' councils to operate at local level looking at issues which are important for them, in their own neighbourhoods. It would then be the responsibility of partnership representatives to assess the relationship of those concerns to the planning issues being addressed by the partnership (and other planning structures) at any one time and to ensure that the concerns were reflected in plans and funding bids. This responsibility would include a duty to give clear feedback to the children and young people about the way in which this process was working.

It is the consideration of mechanisms such as these that will form a part of the ongoing partnership development and plan monitoring work which the Unit will be doing with the local authorities in this project. It will also be an agenda item, although not in so much depth, for the Early Years Coordinators' Network, both in national and regional meetings and in the practice exchange database available through the Internet.

We finish with a quotation from a book on children's rights edited by Brannen and O'Brien (1996):

'Once children are enabled to speak and be heard, we may have to participate in new conversations.'

Our experience from this project would show that you can turn this quotation around and say that children can and do speak now. It is not so much about enabling children to be heard as enabling adults to listen and that this, as well as the setting up of mechanisms, is the big challenge for partnerships.

Appendix 3. Outline of the HERA 2 survey of Early Years Development and Childcare Plans for the Early Years National Training Organisation

Introduction

The report is based on an analysis of 118 of the 150 Early Years Development and Childcare Plans (EYDCPs) which was carried out in March 1999 at the DfEE by the HERA 2 Project on behalf of the Early Years NTO and NCMA. The work was designed to inform the NTO's discussions on the future training and qualification needs of the early years workforce. In addition, NCMA requested some specific information on the incidence of childminding development projects within the plans. Further information on the work can be obtained from those two organisations. This review of plans was supplemented by some information from the audits and from focus group discussions held in all four UK countries, questions for which were informed by the findings of the survey.

Outline of main report

Nature of the plans

Although plans followed the DfEE guidance, they were very different in structure and mainly qualitative in nature. Each partnership, although counted as a single unit is, in fact, very different. There are unitary authorities and county councils as well as London boroughs, all with very different populations and features. Although there was quantitative data relating to audit information and to planned expansion targets, this was presented differently by many partnerships and not all partnerships provided data in each of the areas being studied:

- areas of childcare need;
- the anticipated expansion of the workforce;
- levels of qualifications/training;
- training needs;
- plans to meet training needs;
- overall training and quality strategies;
- evidence of infrastructure support for implementation of the plans, including the development of childminder networks.

Areas of childcare need and anticipated expansion of the workforce

The greatest childcare need mentioned was for out-of-school care with 48.3 per cent of partnerships listing this as a childcare need in the following areas:

- holiday care;
- before-school care;
- after-school care;
- provision for children with special needs.

A total of 25.4 per cent of the partnerships mentioned childminding as being a priority area for expansion, in order to meet identified childcare need. Childminders are envisaged as being able to meet a range of needs including out-of-school care, education, children from birth to age three and childcare for children with special needs.

Smaller numbers of partnerships also listed needs in the following areas:

- 11 to 14-year-olds;
- family support;
- learning support;
- pre-school;
- employer schemes;
- early education.

Increase in childcare places 1999/2000

Sixty-seven per cent of partnerships listed the target number of places they expected to create in the year 1999/2000. The total number of childcare places was 39,226.

Taking the figures as a whole, the major area of expansion was in out-of-school provision (22,467 places), with the majority of provision being developed in clubs. Some partnerships only provided figures for one or two areas of provision.

Partnerships estimated the expected expansion in childcare places over the next three years in different ways. Some partnerships specified the types of provision, while others did not provide such detail. Figures indicate averages of 1,500 places per partnership for out-of-school provision, 500 for pre-school provision and 600 for children from birth to age three. This indicates an average of 2,700 places per partnership overall, and a national total for England of over 400,000 places.

New staff needed

Thirty two per cent of partnerships were able to estimate the numbers of additional staff who would be needed to deliver the expansion in childcare places. Very approximately, this indicates an average increase of 220 staff per partnership who might be expected to provide for between 2,000 and 2,700 extra childcare places. Grossing up these figures suggests that there will be a need for a possible 33,000 staff to provide an additional 300,000 to 400,000 childcare places.

Qualification levels

Twenty-nine per cent of partnerships mentioned low levels of qualification of child-minders as a concern to be addressed through the partnership's work. Levels of qualified childminders varied by partnership from two per cent to 54 per cent as the proportion of qualified childminders. Forty-three per cent of partnerships mentioned qualification levels in the workforce generally and out-of-school workers were the next lowest qualified occupational group, although this too varied from partnership to partnership from 25 per cent to 80 per cent qualified. Qualification levels of day nursery staff were mainly over 80 per cent and qualification levels of pre-school workers were mainly over 60 per cent.

Forty-four per cent of partnerships identified qualification needs in the workforce. Thirty two partnerships indicated a lack of staff with NVQs, eight specifically mentioned NVQ in playwork and another 24 mentioned playwork in general. Considering the anticipated expansion in out-of-school provision, there appears to be an urgent need to ensure the availability of playwork training.

Qualification targets

Eighteen per cent of partnerships have set qualification targets for their workforce to be achieved over the next three to four years. These varied according to the particular needs of the workforce in the partnership area and anticipated resources for training.

Training needs

The majority of partnerships listed the training needs of the workforce. Partnerships took this data from the Local Government Management Board survey, where practitioners identified their own training needs, and also from their own estimates of what training might be needed. It was not always clear what methodology they had used to undertake their own training needs analysis, although some had taken their data from a study of OFSTED and registration and inspection reports. Health and safety training, including first aid and food hygiene, was mentioned most frequently by partnerships, followed by training to work with children with special needs.

Many of the areas mentioned relate to the national occupational standards for the sector, but there are some, such as assertiveness, quality assurance, inter-agency working, management and business skills and legislation, where the link is perhaps not so clear.

Local training and qualifications

The trend for developing local childcare training programmes has already been noted in the Daycare Trust Survey (1999) and the HERA 2 survey of UK training and qualifications (HERA 2 Final Report, 1999). Nine partnerships mentioned locally-accredited courses currently in development to meet training needs, some of which were pre-registration programmes for childminders, whilst 11 partnerships were developing induction programmes targeting all occupational groups in the workforce. Forty partnerships were planning to use locally-recognised training programmes as a basis for partnership training strategies. Sports qualifications and teaching were also mentioned as being important workforce qualifications, and Pre-School Learning Alliance courses were seen as significant in the pre-school sector. A further nine partnerships were planning to ensure that the DCP1 and 2 (the new programmes for childminders) were locally available.

Training strategies

Seventy-one partnerships had developed, or started to develop a training strategy. Strategies were very varied in nature, but the most frequently mentioned components were:
- locally developed, accredited programmes;
- coordination of training providers;
- self-assessment;

- quality and training subgroups of partnerships;
- publication of a comprehensive training directory;
- local forums and cluster groups used for training purposes;
- access to in-service training;
- training for assessors.

Evidence of infrastructure support for implementation of the plans, including the development of childminder networks

Features of capacity building varied widely, although there were some common points:
- development posts;
- development of local forums;
- recruitment of staff/marketing sector;
- resource/toy library;
- sustainability fund;
- service-level agreements with the voluntary sector;
- links with regeneration initiatives;
- development of an integrated service;
- information service/advice line;
- alternative use of premises.

The majority of partnerships were planning to employ development workers to undertake capacity building in a range of ways. Most of these posts were to be established by the local authority, rather than through service-level agreements with the voluntary sector. Local forums, either through school-based networks or existing early years forums were seen as the means of building capacity at local level. Partnerships hoped that access to better resources through libraries would improve quality, and many partnerships were establishing sustainability funds to support failing provision as a means of ensuring viability.

Premises were a concern for a number of partnerships, either because of a lack of suitable ones in urban areas, or because of a lack of any kind of premises in rural areas. Eight partnerships were creating coordinator posts to oversee the implementation of the plan. A few partnerships were exploring the development of an integrated service, but very few made mention of Health Action Zones or Education Action Zones. Only four partnerships noted the lack of provision for minority ethnic children and the need to recruit staff from minority ethnic communities.

Childminder Network Development

There were 65 partnerships who were planning to develop a childminder network, and seven partnerships where there was already one in existence. Just over a half of partnerships in this group were appointing staff to develop such networks. The majority of these new posts appear to be local authority appointments, although 25 per cent of posts were in the form of service-level agreements with the local childminding association. About 10 per cent of partnerships mentioned the NCMA scheme as part of their quality assurance strategy. Childminder networks are being proposed to target the needs of a range of groups of children, as follows:
- specific minority ethnic groups (Chinese, Bangladeshi and Portuguese);
- children with special needs (out-of-school);
- from birth to age three;

- children in need (the majority);
- children out-of-school.

Conclusions

Anticipated expansion of the workforce

The largest area of anticipated expansion is in the out-of-school sector, with holiday care as an important subsection. Significant expansion is anticipated in services for very young children. Childminders are expected to play an important part in the delivery of a wide range of services including education, out-of-school and the care of very young children. There is some evidence that services in some areas will extend hours, in order to offer a more comprehensive service. Few partnerships have targets for employer-based schemes.

Based on data from the plans, the early years workforce could expand by 33,000 in the next three years, providing between 300,000 and 400,000 new childcare places, an average of between 2,000 and 2,700 per partnership.

Levels of qualifications, training needs, plans to meet training needs and overall training and quality strategies

There are some significant training needs which have been identified by partnerships, many of whom are planning programmes to address those needs. In particular, playwork training, training for childminders, training for people working with children under three and children with special needs will be a priority, although a range of other needs have been identified. There are some questions which need to be considered here:

- There is a national framework for training and qualifications currently in development, but will it be able to meet the relevant needs?
- The national occupational standards cover some of the identified areas, but there are specific skills and competencies needed by the new development workers in the early years sector which are not included. Other areas, which are central to the new way of working defined by the National Childcare Strategy, such as locality-based planning, business planning and working across sectors, are not in the national occupational standards.
- Partnerships are seeking forms of endorsement for continuing professional development.
- There are two National Training Organisations in the sector who are developing endorsement systems, but will these be accessible for partnerships currently planning training programmes, and will there be transferability and equivalency between the two systems to facilitate endorsement for multidisciplinary programmes?
- Partnerships which are currently developing induction/orientation courses may be duplicating the forthcoming national course, proposed as part of the QCA framework.
- There will be a significant need for NVQ assessment centres. There are indications from partnerships and the Further Education Funding Council that there may not be enough assessment centres offering NVQs, especially the playwork NVQ, to provide sufficient access to these qualifications for practitioners. Specific work needs to be done on mapping provision to ensure national availability.
- Partnerships have spent time and energy on developing locally-accredited courses, which a significant number see as central to their training strategies. How will partnerships link these to the national training and qualifications framework, and

how can NTOs working on national planning ensure that this desire for local programmes is incorporated into national strategies?

- There is no standard way of assessing training need in the childcare sector. Guidance could usefully provide a structure for this in the future.
- There is a range of quality assurance schemes available to partnerships and a number which are being developed in the form of a local kitemark by individual partnerships. Whilst this indicates a clear commitment to quality standards, there is no means of measuring the equivalence of quality assurance schemes. Without national guidance in this area, there is a danger of inconsistency and confusion.
- Work on training strategies is patchy. There are few links made between the development of quality standards and training strategies.
- There is a need for training at a strategic level to support partnerships to undertake some of their tasks, in particular: linking with other local and national initiatives; working across sectors; capacity building; training needs analysis; and development of cross-sector quality standards.

Evidence of infrastructure support for implementation of the plans, including the development of childminder networks

A significant number of partnerships are creating development worker posts to support capacity building. Many of these are local authority appointments, rather than being created through service-level agreements with the voluntary sector. Little detail was provided to suggest how recruitment of staff, particularly childminders, might take place, yet the role of childminders within plans is often key to capacity building. The complexities of childminder recruitment should not be underestimated, and more work could usefully be done to provide guidance in this area.

Local forums are seen as playing an important part in local capacity building, but there are few examples of good practice within the new context of locality planning and consultation, which could provide guidance as to how these could work most successfully.

There is little evidence in the plans of links with other key government initiatives which impact on children such as Quality Protects, Health and Education Action Zones and economic development initiatives in general. There is a need for information about these other initiatives to be circulated to partnerships, and for specific information to be included in the guidance in order for these links to be made more effectively.

Finally, there is little consistency in the way in which plans are written and presented and, in many cases, data presented by partnerships was inconsistent between sections in the plans. For future research purposes, and in order to identify national trends, it might be helpful to give more detailed guidance on presentation of quantitative and qualitative data in the plans, by providing the types of tables and spreadsheets which, for example, the European Social Fund Unit provides.

Appendix 4. Issues arising at the national meeting of the Early Years Coordinators' Network with Margaret Hodge, Minister for Education, 21 June 1999

Prior to the Minister's arrival, the meeting agreed on seven main areas for discussion, each of which would be introduced by a nominated speaker who would then be supported by others.

Acknowledgment of the network as a forum for continuing dialogue with central government

- It was suggested that partnerships felt a bit marginalised. National organisations produce glossy leaflets, but the local perspective is being left out. This point was made positively: partnerships are a resource, not victims.
- Don't duplicate meetings: if there's a good network already (such as this one), use that rather than setting up a new one. However, it was recognised that Chairs of Partnerships might need to meet separately.
- Sometimes existing forums aren't listened to.
- Deliverability depends on the people in this room not on the people the Government is talking to at national level. This is a real issue in terms of the revised targets.
- Perhaps we could arrange a series of seminars with the key civil servants on the issues raised today.
- Importance of the links with other partnerships and locality developments in the regions; the network can support this.
- Make the point that, despite the timescales and difficulties, there are many positive examples.

The Minister said that they recognised that these were the people who made the strategy deliverable and were grateful for all the hard work of officers and partnerships. They would be very willing to meet again, regularly, to continue the dialogue around specific issues.

Links and connections

- Questions have been responded to differently by the DfEE and the New Opportunities Fund (NOF). Could there be some liaison and consistency?
- A lot of time has been lost in the bureaucracy of contracting and NOF criteria over the last three months, so there's a danger of having lower rather than higher targets.

- It would help to have improved connections with other organisations involved in delivering the National Childcare Strategy, for example NOF, in order to create more responsive and coordinated timescales. Local planning regimes also need to be contacted by central government as they are sometimes asking for inappropriate requirements to be met by small providers and this could hold up the process of creating places. Also, large national chains of providers are bypassing the partnerships in some areas, which also affects their ability to deliver a coherent local strategy. These are examples of national planning tasks which only central government can sort out.

The Minister said that there had been a misunderstanding about the NOF deadlines and that the information on them had been badly expressed originally. It was perfectly possible to send in applications at any time, not necessarily by the deadline dates. These dates are only a reference point for NOF who have agreed to turn around applications within four months of each deadline. She intends to meet with NOF to clarify the problems.

The Minister's meeting with NOF revealed that the deadlines were, in fact, as originally stated, the dates by which applications were to be received. NOF subsequently agreed to meet with the Coordinators' Network to discuss issues and this meeting was held on 27 July 1999.

The Minister also agreed to look into the issue of what could be done about local planning requirements and the national nursery chains.

Regulation and quality control

- They would like to know something specific on the timetable for this, following last year's consultation document.
- They felt concerned about precipitate legislation on changes in regulation without adequate consultation.
- They expressed concerns about early learning goals and on what they are based. It was felt that the QCA's response to their consultation exercise on the Desirable Learning Outcomes did not take the concerns of managers and practitioners seriously.
- They felt there was a danger of lowering of standards for out-of-school provision for children over eight. How will accreditation for NOF and Working Families' Tax Credit (WFTC) purposes be handled to avoid this?
- They thought there was real difficulty in recruiting to registration and inspection units when morale is so low. There might be no-one to register the new provision.

The Minister said that the changes in the regulatory and inspection framework would be out very soon and that they would represent the final version, so essentially the consultation process had finished. The new guidance on Early Years Development Plans would explain the process by which agencies could register to deliver the accreditation process for groups caring only for children over the age of eight and this process should be in place by April 2000.

Use of the audits

- There is a lack of recognition by central government of the findings of the audits. Targets were built on those findings but partnerships are now being asked to revise them.

- How do we respond to the Government's own need to meet targets? This needs to be acknowledged at the same time as stressing that places also have to be sustainable in order to meet these targets.
- There is a worry that there is no real concern from the Government over quality and sustainability, especially in rural areas.
- Under the present system, local authorities venture money into the community which might not get paid back by the DfEE, if groups can't produce places.
- There is real concern about the quarterly reports to the DfEE. If actual places created are really the only way to trigger repayment, then there will be serious difficulties in covering costs because of the time needed to get the capacity building strategies up and running.
- There needs to be more recognition of the local agenda and how working on that will help to bring about trust within the partnerships and promote partnership development.
- The positive achievements in partnership development need to be stressed. *This is going well if it is left alone.* There is also real creativity, but this is often not recognised and it is not being nourished in a systematic and detailed way. For example, members would like more information on the research into the effectiveness of partnerships. It was felt that partnerships would like some input into the research process; things which they feel it would be useful to look at.
- Partnership development needs considerable time in order to build on existing networks in an area and to consolidate relationships.
- Local authority areas differ considerably in size, but the work remains the same for partnerships and local authority officers.
- It was accepted that the DfEE was putting national investment into partnership development, but it seems to be ignoring existing forums such as this in order to set up new things. Why is this?

Margaret Hodge said that the targets were not going to be changed and that partnerships must do their best to meet them and try hard to exceed them. She pointed out that not all partnerships had been asked to increase their targets. A draft of the revised guidance is due to be given to Ms Hodge before the end of July 1999 and will then be issued to partnerships prior to final publication in September 1999.

Recruitment and retention

- Recruitment and retention of staff is a real problem. This is true at all levels, for local authority officers, for development workers and for actual providers.
- There is some danger of deskilling within voluntary organisations and a subsequent difficulty in retaining staff.
- Training implications are enormous and require funding on the scale given to the numeracy and literacy initiatives.
- Issue of threatened resignations in partnerships through target revision, sustainability, and so on.

Ms Hodge noted the group's concern over low gradings of early years development and coordinator posts and the lack of understanding of the coordinator/partnership officer role which this low status reflected. However, she said this was a local authority responsibility over which she could have no control. In connection with short-term contracts for development officers, she stressed that this is a five-year strategy with funding secured for at least the first three years, so this should not be a problem.

Accountability, responsibility and legality

- The areas of accountability, responsibility and legality are very contradictory and confused at present. Clarity would help partnerships and local authorities. In some places, it feels that there is less coordination now partly because of the above. Many representations have been made to the DfEE about this and it has been noted by the Audit Commission. Elected members are also raising this issue in their forums.
- People feel achievement in their new plans, so it will be very undermining to have new guidance issued now.
- Finding the Revenue Support Grant money proved to be a real problem this year. Could it be clearly located and quantified?
- Early years is now at the forefront of planning processes, but the support/ infrastructure for it is not keeping up. It is still a Cinderella service, especially when compared with Education Plans and Quality Protects, for instance.

There was surprise from both the Minister and civil servants at the legality/accountability issue and it was agreed that a small group from this meeting would meet as a matter of urgency with the Childcare Unit to look at this issue before the draft guidance is completed.

A group of volunteers was convened for this meeting which was subsequently held on 7 July 1999 with Sue Archer and Nick Tooze of the DfEE, and the following points emerged:

- Last year there had been a deliberate policy to be vague over the role of the partnerships but, in reality, their only role (as specified in the School Standards and Framework Act) is an advisory one. It is the duty of the local authority to establish and service the partnerships, complete the audits and plans, meet the targets within them, report on a quarterly basis to the DfEE and be accountable for the funding. A diagrammatic representation of the accountability structure would be included in the new guidance. However, it was felt very important that the role of the partnerships should not be devalued. Their role in the context of Best Value and the modernisation of local government had not been considered in this guidance.
- Partnerships were not a legal entity which could employ development workers. However, the coordinators' delegation pointed out that there would be ways around this, such as establishing them as development trusts along the lines of other regeneration partnerships.
- One issue which had been looked at in connection with the redraft of the guidance was that of admissions and point of entry to school, but it had been decided that the DfEE was not in a position to do anything about this centrally.

Following the Minister's visit, there was a general discussion and debriefing which also included the following points:

- Half those present had replied to the DfEE's request for increased targets by saying that they would not alter them. What would be the effect of this?
- It was noted that the Sure Start thinking is very different, with much more recognition of capacity building.
- The outcomes of children having poor quality or non-sustainable places could be perverse in that they could prove to be *poorer* learners in the future.
- Inappropriate national targets have been sold both to DfEE and to the Treasury who are driving the DfEE's targets. It would be helpful to invite the Treasury to a future meeting, in order to give some more realistic information and discuss the issue of sustainability.

- There must also be a public service contract for the National Childcare Strategy, similar to the one for Sure Start, and it would be interesting to see this.
- It was noted that the current situation caused difficulties for councillors who wish to support the Labour Party targets.
- Try to get children back into the discussion. Members of this network are supposed to know about children's needs, but they too easily get left out of the discussion.
- We should provide the Minister with more examples of good practice, because she criticised the quality of relationships between social services and LEAs and the involvement of the private and voluntary sector.
- She had been positive about the role of childminders and noted that we hadn't mentioned them, but it must be recognised that childminders are not as easy to recruit as might be imagined.
- Seminar suggestions for future consultation meetings should include:
  - accountability, responsibility and legality within the context of Best Value;
  - regulation and inspection and their connection to quality, within the context of the Early Learning Goals;
  - links and connections with other organisations, for example, NOF and local planning regimes;
  - services for three-year-olds;
  - sustainability of out-of-school provision;
  - recruitment and retention of staff.

References

Alderson, P (1995) *Listening to Children: Children, ethics and social research.* Barnardo's

Aldgate, J and Tunstill, J (1994) *Implementing Section 17 of the Children Act: The first 18 months. A study for the Department of Health.* Leicester University

Audit Commission (1994) *Seen But Not Heard: Coordinating community child health and social services for children in need. Detailed evidence and guidelines for managers and practitioners.* HMSO

Audit Commission (1996) *Counting to Five: Education of children under five.* HMSO

Ball, C (1994) *Start Right: The importance of early learning.* Royal Society for the Encouragement of Arts, Manufactures and Commerce

Barber, M (1996) *The Learning Game: Arguments for an education revolution.* Gollancz

Brannen, J and O'Brien, M eds (1996) *Children in Families: Research and policy.* Falmer Press

Bullock, R and others (1995) *Child Protection: Messages from research.* HMSO

Butler-Sloss, E (1988) *Report of the Inquiry into Child Abuse in Cleveland 1987.* HMSO

Central Advisory Council for Education (England) (1967) *Children and their Primary Schools. A report of the CACE (The Plowden Report) Vol. 1: Report. Vol. 2: Research and surveys.* HMSO

Children Act 1989. HMSO

Childcare Audit 1999/2000 (1999) *Sefton Early Years and Childcare Partnership*

Connor, E (1971) *Projectile. A summary of the Liverpool EPA 1968–1971.* Liverpool EPA Publications

Cordeaux, C and others (1999) *Childcare Training in the UK: Final report of the HERA 2 project.* Suffolk Social Services

Dahlberg, G, Moss, P and Pence, A (1999) *Beyond Quality in Early Childhood Education and Care: Postmodern perspectives.* Falmer Press

Department for Education and Employment (1996) *Work and Family: Ideas and options for childcare. A consultation paper.* DfEE

Department for Education and Employment (1997) *Early Years Development Partnerships and Plans. Guidance 1998–99.* DfEE

Department for Education and Employment (1998a) *Early Years Development and Childcare Partnership Planning Guidance 1999–2000.* DfEE

Department for Education and Employment (1998b) *Meeting the Childcare Challenge. A framework and consultation document.* DfEE

Department for Education and Employment (1999a) *Early Years Development and Childcare Partnership Planning Guidance 2000–2001*. DfEE

Department for Education and Employment (1999b) *Summary of the Responses to the Consultation Paper on the Regulation of Early Education and Day Care*. DfEE

Department for Education and Employment (1999c) '£30 million for thousands more nursery staff for safer, better nurseries – Hodge' (Press Release 371/99 2 August). DfEE

Department for Education and Employment and Department of Health (1998) *Consultation Paper on the Regulation of Early Education and Day Care*. DfEE/DoH

Department of Education and Science (1972) *Education: A framework for expansion*. Cmnd 5174. HMSO

Department of Education and Science (1990) *Starting with Quality: The report of the Committee of Inquiry into the quality of educational experience offered to 3- and 4-year-olds*. HMSO

Department of Education and Science and Welsh Office (1973) *Nursery Education*. DES Circular 2/73, Welsh Office Circular 39/73. DES/Welsh Office

Department of Health (1990) *Children's Day Care Facilities at 31 March 1990, England*. A/F 90/6

Department of Health (1991) *The Children Act 1989 Guidance and Regulations. Vol. 2 – Family support, day care and educational provision for young children*. HMSO

Elfer, P and Beasley, G (1997) *A Law Unto Themselves? A survey of appeals and prosecutions under Part X of the Children Act 1989, concerning childminding and day care provision*. National Children's Bureau

Hevey, D (1987) *The Continuing Under Fives Muddle! An investigation of current training opportunities*. VOLCUF

HM Treasury (1998) *Comprehensive Spending Review. Cross-departmental review of provision for young children: supporting papers*. HM Treasury

House of Commons Education, Science and Arts Committee (1988) *Educational Provision for the Under Fives*. HMSO

House of Commons Social Services Committee (1984) *Children in Care: Second report, Session 1983–84*. HMSO

Hurd, T, Lerner, R and Barton, C (1999) 'Integrated services: expanding partnerships to meet the needs of today's children and families', *Young Children*, 54, 2, 74–80

Kids' Clubs Network (1999) *The Childcare Revolution. Facts and figures for 1998*. KCN

Labour Party (1996) *Early Excellence: A head start for every child*. The Labour Party

London Borough of Sutton (1999) *Early Years Development and Childcare Plan*.

Lowndes, V and Riley, K (1994) *Coordinating Services for Young Children: The implication for management*. Local Government Management Board Alderson, P (1995) *Listening to Children: Children, ethics and social research*. Barnardo's

McQuail, S and Pugh, G (1995) *The Effective Organisation of Early Childhood Services*. National Children's Bureau

Meadow Lake Tribal Council and University of Victoria: School of Child and Youth Care (undated) *Children are our Future. Curriculum development project*. Canada: UVIC and MLTC

Ministry of Housing and Local Government (1968) *Report of the Committee on Local Authority and Allied Personal Social Services. (The Seebohm Report)* HMSO (Cmnd 3703)

Moss, P and Penn, H (1996) *Transforming Nursery Education*. Paul Chapman Publishing

Municipality of Reggio Emilia – Infant-Toddler Centres and Preschools (1996) *Catalogue of the Exhibition 'The Hundred Languages of Children'*. Reggio Children

New, R (1998) 'Reggio Emilia's commitment to children and community: a reconceptualisation of quality and DAP' *Early Years*, 18, 2, 11–18

Owen, R (1836) *A New View of Society, and Other Writings*. 1927 edition. Everyman Library

Owen, S and McQuail, S (1997) Learning from Vouchers: An evaluation of phase one of the vouchers scheme for four-year-olds, 1996/97. National Children's Bureau

Pearce, J (1993) *At the Heart of the Community Economy*. Calouste Gulbenkian Foundation

PEEP (1995) *The Peers Early Education Partnership Development Plan*. The PEEP Centre, Peers School, Sandy Lane West, Littlemore, Oxford OX4 5JY

Pence, A and McCallum, M 'Developing cross-cultural partnerships: implications for childcare quality research and practice' in Moss, P and Pence, A eds (1994) *Valuing Quality in Early Childhood Services*. Paul Chapman Publishing

Qualifications and Curriculum Authority (1999a) *The Review of the Desirable Outcomes for Children's Learning on Entering Compulsory Education*. QCA

Qualifications and Curriculum Authority (1999b) *Review of the Desirable Outcomes for Children's Learning on Entering Compulsory Education: Preliminary consultation outcomes*. QCA

Rees, J (1999) *Sure Start Trailblazer Application*. Blackpool Social Services

School Standards and Framework Act 1998. TSO

Scottish Office (1998) *Guidance on the Planning of Pre-school Education and Childcare and the Establishment of Childcare Partnerships*. Scottish Office

Smith, A (1996) *Incorporating Children's Perspectives into Research: Challenge and opportunity*. Keynote address at the New Zealand Association for Research in Education Annual Conference, December 1995

Sure Start (1999) *Trailblazer Conference, 7 July 1999. Report*. Sure Start

Sylva, K and others (1999) *The Effective Provision of Pre-school Education Project. Introduction to EPPE*. [Working Paper no. 1] University of London, Institute of Education

van der Eyken, W ed (1973) *Education, the Child and Society: A documentary history*. Penguin Books

van der Eyken, W (1987) *The DHSS Under-fives Initiative 1983–1987. Final report*. DHSS

Index